MW00626396

FREE YOUR REAL VISION

Release Your Fears, Achieve Your Goals,

Transform Your Life

Gina,
    I hope this gift inspires your future work and further motivates you to continue to encourage and uplift others. Happy Birthday, sis!
            Love,
            Alosho

Alexandria B. Harris

ALEXANDRIA BARABIN HARRIS

Copyright © 2020 by Alexandria Patrice Barabin Harris

All rights reserved. This book or any portion thereof may not be reproduced or used in any manner whatsoever without the express written permission of the publisher except for the use of brief quotations in a book review. Any internet addresses or organization names in this book are offered as a resource. They are not intended in any way to be or imply an endorsement.

Printed in the United States of America

First Printing, 2020

ISBN 978-0-578-69505-1

Yes She Leads Publishing

Atlanta, GA

www.YesSheLeads.com

TABLE OF CONTENTS

PREFACE

D
ear heart, loved one, sister friend of mine, I need you to hear something, whether you are hearing it for the first time, or it is a reminder to your soul. You ready? You are worthy of the vision God gave you and placed in your heart. Choose faith over fear, let go, and stop holding back. Get ready to unleash your vision. It's time to get free.

It is time to embrace your creative brilliance, master the message that will help you serve at a higher level, and seize the opportunities that grant you access to your real vision. After years of hosting vision board workshops for sister circles, church conferences, and women leaders, I want more women to confidently embrace an authentic vision for her life. The journey requires you to get to know who you really are and do the inner work to show up fully present in your experience of life.

Show up and shine bright! It is just that simple. But just because it is simple doesn't mean it is easy. Life's experiences can challenge your growth, and the momentum can fade. That's why it is so important that you look at vision differently than what is commonly discussed: the material and the artificial. You need authentic transformation. You need a real vision for your life. Now is the season for this. The world is shifting right before our eyes every single day in these uncertain times. There has been a collective reality check about what is most important and how quickly it all can fade: career, status, health, and life itself. The shift is happening from excessive to just the essentials, a pivot from quantity to quality. It's a new dawn and a new day. This book is here to help you take what you need to learn (or unlearn) in this season and integrate it into your life. God directed me to write the book I needed for myself so many years ago, full of reality checks and reminders. Real vision must become an active part of your journey because you are a vision in progress. Embrace the gifts of imperfection. Cultivate what matters most. Celebrate your authentic life. It is time to get free. Let's go!

Chapter 1

REAL VISION FOR REAL LIFE

"Just living is not enough,' said the butterfly. One must have sunshine, freedom, and a little flower."
-Hans Christian Anderson, The Butterfly[i]

Falling in love

Giving birth

Witnessing baptism

Performing poetry on stage to a live audience

Roaming city streets at midnight with my dearest friends

The 2009 Inauguration

Singing in the church choir

Traveling to a new place

Any time a yellow butterfly unexpectedly crosses my path

These are moments that have transformed me and the vision I have for my life. However, the unlikely experience that transformed my perspective on vision the most came from sitting in Row 12 Seat C of an airplane from New York to Los Angeles looking out the window as the pilot prepared to descend. 20,000 feet. The clouds dissipate and the luscious mountain landscapes are in full view. Now, 10,000 feet. Here, the landscape of the ground below looks like a patchwork quilt with various shades of the same color. The darker green you can make out to be forest or lush farmland. The lighter green is acres of grass. Then 5,000 feet is where you can make out which direction cars are driving on the freeway. You can recognize city sky lines and famous buildings that easily tower over anyone standing at the front doors. Before you know it, you've landed, coming face to face with the world at your eye level, the way you see it every single day. It is to scale. It is reality.

The highest sky view represents your life, an overarching view of everything you have and hope to accomplish in your lifetime. It is massive and wide. Hundreds of experiences, thousands of days, and millions of minutes captured in one unique life. Yours. As you journey closer, the details become clearer. This is where your real vision lives. It is still a wide view of life but with specific objectives, long-term goals that will take time to accomplish. It is what you dream, desire, and decide to do by taking action. You can see them clearly but perhaps they remain out of reach. Yet, you know that is where you ultimately want to be, even if you are not exactly sure how to get there. You build the road by walking in faith anyway.

That last look around before you touch down is in line with your short-term goals; the things you know need to be done in order for you to move forward over the next coming weeks, months, or the year. You know exactly what it is and where it is. You have the deadlines scheduled in your planner. You know what time it is.

But the minute you touch the ground, the view immediately changes. You land in the thick of it. The day to day of it all. It is the to-do list, the habits, the daily interruptions, the unexpected emergencies where you drop everything because nothing is going according to plan.

Vision lives in the alignment between the ground and the sky; between the everydayness of daily life and the future in your vision that may be years away. The problem is many people stay on one extreme or the other. In Camp A- you have the folks who shout at the top of their lungs "Expand your vision! Enlarge your vision!" to anyone who will listen. Yet, if you asked them what they are doing today to make progress towards that vision, a hush falls upon them. Suddenly, they are all too quiet. And then there is Camp B. These well-meaning and often hard-working folks can only deal with the deeds of the day, rarely taking a birds-eye view of the bigger picture, often thinking that walking in vision is idealistic and unattainable.

Being stuck in the future, able to see but unable to do and being stuck in your present only able to see what is right in front of you leaves you in the same place: stuck. Allow me to offer an alternative. To successfully walk, live, and move in your vision, it requires the collaboration between the daily habits, such as the short-term goals, and the forecasting that is part of long-term vision. Real vision is the common ground between reality and your lifetime goals. It is a combination of 1) you deciding to live your values, taking authentic and intentional action; 2) the opportunities presented by those who are willing to support and invest in you; and 3) the divine pathways that are revealed to you along your journey.

Now, before you start with that "I'm just a regular person and I don't really have some special vision," let me pause you right there. Yes girl, you do! But perhaps it is not accessible to you. Not yet. It is bound up in myths, stereotypes, disappointments, and unmet expectations. It is hiding out behind the heartbreak, rejection, and pain of the past. Perhaps it is buried under the stress of a broken marriage, chronic health issues, or financial debt. Beyond those tears and behind those years, your real vision is still within you. It's time to free your real vision.

To free your vision means to do any of the following in order for your vision to have the space it needs to be activated in your life:

Release it.

Unleash it.

Unmask it.

Uncover it.

Discover it.

Reveal it.

Heal it.

Seek it.

Speak it.

Grow it.

Show it.

Breathe it.

Give it.

Live it.

You have a powerful voice in the world, yet you whisper. It is time to speak up, speak out, and speak now instead of holding back, hiding your many gifts, and ideas in the shadows of your daily life. Stop playing small, avoiding the vision you have been given. It is time to be brave. Summon all the courage you need to take the next step, even if that means you must do it afraid because fear is not the problem. Yes, it is a challenge to overcome, but the real problem is deeper than the fear. The threat to your growth is when doubt is allowed to stop you from facing your fears and opens the door for isolation, indecision, and confusion. Instead of making progress, you feel paralyzed. For many, this is where the journey to vision ends. It's not because a person isn't willing to work hard, or that they are not good enough to make it happen. It is often because they felt discouraged and defeated. As a result, they did not take the next step forward and stopped making progress. They got stuck. They gave up.

But you are not giving up. Not today! I know this because you are here, reading this book. Maybe you were stuck in the past, but you know that God can make all things new. So, here you are. You are pushing past the negative self-talk, the imposter syndrome, and the limiting beliefs because you have a genuine desire to live a life of authenticity. You are taking the necessary steps to breathe new life into your vision. Baby steps or giant steps; either way, it doesn't matter which kind of step you take because they are all steps. Little by little over time becomes a lot more than no action at all. What matters is you are making progress, and that is something to be proud of.

As a matter of fact, today is a giant step for you. Believe it or not, you are already in conversation with your real vision which may be why this topic interest you in the first place. You have tried the vision board parties, attended the magical retreat, or the information packed conference only to return home and feel that momentum waning. Yet, you long to be back in a clear space of belonging where you seek what you speak, putting actions behind your vision and goals. It is part of you, part of your story, crafted from the very fabric of your life experience. You want the lessons and the blessings.

The reminder is necessary. Often, as precious, and impressionable young girls, society teaches her that being special has more to do with looks, good hair, or her grades are rather than her character, her creativity or compassion for others. As adults, a woman's worth is debated based on her ability to attract men, to have children and walk the fine and judgmental line between being a gold-digger way over town and the I-N-D-E-P-E-N-D-E-N-T because you know what that means; she got her own house and her own car. She is constantly judged by how she speaks and the way she looks. Speak too softly and someone might try to walk all over her like a doormat, taking her kindness for weakness. Speak too boldly and they will call her loud, or "aggressive," for doing the same thing a man would be rewarded as an "assertive" go-getter for doing. We learn to censor our thoughts. We learn to filter our words. We learn to turn down our dreams and turn up the fantasy.

Women are taught to pursue admiration, approval, and validation ra-ther than vision, dreams, and goals.

With all of that noise, you may have learned to ignore your vision in order to blend in and not be so different from everyone else. Perhaps you've been told one-too many times that you just can't do it. At one point in time, insecurity and heart break broke your spirit in more ways than one. Then, there was that time you gathered up your courage to ask for the help and support you needed. And when you did not receive it, that experience taught you to hide instead of hope. The good news is the seeds of your vision are part of you. They are still there to be uncovered or unmasked waiting to be revealed. Left unattended and neglected, however, your vision will remind you that it is still there, ready whenever you are.

Is your vision politely asking, "Where are you going?" like a sweet old neighbor waving from across the street? Or is it like a screaming new-born child demanding a response? Regardless of the frequency, you are being called to be a visionary. You have been led to this moment right here, right now for a reason. What is being called forth in your life right now? What do you feel compelled to do?

I spent years without a real vision. After a few challenging years re-building and totally reimagining my life after all of it hit the fan, I spent time figuring out who I was and who I was going to be once the dust settled. I began to ask God for clarity and direction. I started sift-ing through my life, from childhood to the present, searching for "the real me." I began paying attention to the reoccurring themes, the gifts and talents that served others well, and the activities that brought me joy. For the first time in my life, I acknowledged the things that came natural to me as perhaps a clue about my direction and appreciating the fact that God created me to be unique. Then, I finally made the connection that if everything God does has a purpose, then my life had a purpose as well. That epiphany helped me reexamine my experience with fresh eyes and new perspective in order to see how it cleared the path on the journey towards my vision. Pain turned into purpose; isolation turned into incubation; and grief became growth.

Those years of personal and spiritual growth during my time as a single woman traveling the country, pursuing my own version of success made a significant difference in my life. It served to clear so much clutter from my soul in preparation for what was next to come. A husband, a daughter, a house, and two businesses later, I was able to reflect on that time in my life and reap the benefits of transforming my mess into a message.

After becoming a mom, I decided that rather than return to full-time work, I would instead pursue full-time entrepreneurship. I began hosting workshops annually, traveling to cities across the country, training, and engaging women on the topics of vision, leadership, culture, and empowerment. This book was written in that same spirit; to create a safe space of support that empowers women like you: women of community, faith, and culture who are learning to embrace authenticity over insecurity; progress above perfection, and faith more than fear. I want to talk to the woman who has been deeply wounded by toxic relationships and left feeling rejection, shame, or deep seeded doubt behind what someone else has said or done to her. hindered in the past by a lack of support and lack of clarity. It's time to take your vision from artificial to authentic and from ordinary to extraordinary! You are an amazing, talented visionary leader full of life. Free your vision so that it may reflect that beautiful light.

Reality Check Your Vision: What does the title of this book "Free Your Real Vision" mean to you? What are you hoping to learn by reading this book?

Circle one of the options below. How are you planning to take notes while you read?

Take Notes in a Journal

Take Notes on My Phone

Take Notes by the Margins of the Book

Chapter 2

VISION BEYOND THE BOARD

You can create the most perfect vision board, but it doesn't mean you have a perfect path to your vision. The goal is inspiration, not imitation. You are the real thing.
#FreeYourRealVision
-Alexandria @YesSheLeads

R eady to create a vision board? It's a simple process really. Get a few of your favorite magazines laying around the house. Make a quick run to the craft store and pick up some scissors, glue, and a poster board of your choice. They have quite a selection. You can use a standard white cardboard. Perhaps you want to jazz it up with a colorful selection. There are tri-fold presentation boards; boards with adhesive on the back so you can easily post it to the wall in your home or office. Ok, once you have all of your supplies, that's pretty much it. You're all set. Except for one minor detail. Where is your vision?! It is not a supply you can pick up from the store like everything else. And please don't depend on the magazines to bring it to you. They are beautiful and inspiring; but remember they sell ads, not vision. So where exactly do you get your vision for the vision board? When do you focus on your real vision, an authentic vision, in order to create an authentic vision board? Questions that need answers.

When you think about making a vision board, is the vision you have for your giant life at the center of it? Or is it more of an after-thought? Instead of a vision board, which of the following do you have?

A) a shopping board
B) a wish board
C) a fantasy board

Or is it a poster of the prettiest pictures you could find in Essence and Oprah magazine? Most vision boards are projections of what people may dream of without any real connection to what they work towards. Some vision boards are just pretty pictures that represent what society tells women to focus on: romantic fantasies and shopping. But you can't buy someone else's vision and slap it on a board, hoping it sticks without the glue. Surprise! The plot twist is that you are the glue.

Honestly, I love vision boards. They are a fun and effective way to get my creative juices flowing and help me use my imagination. In fact, vision boards have played a role in my life quite a few times. Making a vision board has helped me set goals and plan for the future. It is what has led me on this journey to help women use vision boards to plan for a giant life. As a woman who is over six feet tall, I have been called a giant many times, and I didn't always take kindly to those words. But now, I embrace it! Yes, I am a giant, and I want all of us to have a giant life; a life that is so spacious that you can stretch all the way out like extra legroom and an empty row to yourself on a long flight. Your giant life is abundant and overflowing with possibilities and opportunities. There is room to breathe, to stretch, to grow into your vision. Your giant life is not solely focused on things. Your attitude, your stress level, your openness to change, and your values matter as well. When you embrace your giant life, you can also embrace the giant difference you can make. When was the last time you were asked to capture that on a vision board? You get to define what a giant life is for you. Need some help on where to start? Focus on the overarching themes that encompass success in all important areas over the course of your life, spiritual, personal, and professional.

A vision is not just one picture or singular image of who you "should" become. It is much more like a mosaic, all these smaller lovely images and snapshots of your life that are brought together to create one big picture. This is why vision boards are such a popular and accessible way to talk about vision. However, there are some missing ingredients that are key to vision board success. There is so much attention focused on creating a beautiful vision board and not enough focus on creating a beautiful vision.

Let me keep it real. A vision board without a real vision sucks. It's not personal. It's not progressive. It's not authentic. Without a vision, it may be pretty, but it's ineffective in being a tool that supports your goals. When you include vision in your vision board, you take it from ordinary to extraordinary. I have been to vision board parties that didn't actually help me focus on vision at all. I felt like it was a missed opportunity because those gatherings are such an important time for women to come together, celebrate one another, and collectively stretch towards a greater purpose. I love being in community with empowering women who encourage others and lift as they climb. Based on my journey, this book is filled with resources and tools that will help you get more from your vision board whether you are designing it independently or as part of a collective. But first, let's dig deeper into vision.

Now is the perfect time to craft your real vision, not just your vision board. Here are my top three reasons why most vision boards are ordinary instead of extraordinary:

1. **No vision.** A vision board with no vision is bound to feel like a left-over art project in the back of the closet a month after it's made. It's just a bunch of pretty pictures with little to no meaning behind them. A typical vision board includes familiar topics like career, travel, clothes, money, and love. Consider what your short term and long-term goals in these areas to help craft your vision. Ask yourself: What are my values? What is the vision I have for my giant life? What do I hope to accomplish 5 years, 10 years, 20 years from now? That includes external success but also internal mastery. What is the message I want to share with the world? Who is the community that I want to serve? How can I grow spiritually every day? What inspires me to create? As a result, your vision board will be personal, powerful, and purposeful. If you feel like something is missing

from your vision board, it's not about finding another magazine. It's about leading a life you love and finding ways to represent that value on the page. It's about personal growth. An authentic vision reflects deeply who you are and what is in your heart to contribute to the world.

2. **Not Personalized.** When you sit down to do a vision board, your vision helps you make a personal connection to those images. In other words, make it authentic. Many vision boards focus on losing weight, falling in love, or making more money. That's a start. But you are not on the exact same journey as everyone else. Personalize your vision board by digging deeper into the details and understanding your "why?" Ask yourself "why do I want this?" "What is the purpose of putting this on my vision board?" The objectives can sound similar, but your reasons will be different from everyone else. A vision board is an opportunity to really create something just as unique as you are. Romantic relationships are important, but take a look at other relationships too. What about including your vision for your friendships? What would you like family relationships to look and feel like? Capture your journey for inner peace, self-compassion, and grace. You can include your self-care practices, too. Don't be afraid to make it personal.

3. **Not Often Enough**. Vision boards are most popular in January. Why? Yes, it's the start of a new year. But calendars govern holidays and work schedules. Calendars do not govern your vision. The purpose and wisdom required for you to live your vision needs to be accessible to you all year-around. Sure, January is a good time to create a vision board, but so is 6 months later in June. Or your birthday. Or a quiet self-care Saturday after brunch is a great option, too. Stop waiting for a single date on the calendar to spend time cultivating your vision. Vision,

purpose, and wisdom are necessary every day. Thinking of your vision board as a one-time annual project is limiting because vision is year around. When used regularly, a vision board can serve as a symbol to remind you of who you are and who you are becoming.

Now that you are clear on what a real vision board is and is not, it will also help to be clear on what vision is and what it is not. In the next chapter we will dive in to defining real vision.

Reality Check Your Vision: Do you enjoy creating vision boards?

If yes, what do you enjoy about the process? Although you like them, what is one thing you would like to change?

If no, what don't you enjoy about the process? Although you don't enjoy making them, what is one thing you can at least appreciate about vision boards?

Chapter 3

REALITY CHECK: REAL VISION IS, REAL VISION AIN'T

"If you wish to move mountains tomorrow, you must start by lifting stones today."
– African Proverb

According to the dictionary[ii], vision means a) the faculty or state of being able to see; b) the ability to think about or plan the future with imagination or wisdom. Real vision is the language I use to expand on that definition to serve as a connection between today and tomorrow; between here and there; between where you are and where you are going. As I said in Chapter 1, real vision is the common ground between today's reality and your lifetime goals. It is a combination of 1) you deciding to live your values, taking authentic and intentional action; 2) the opportunities presented by those who are willing to support and invest in you; and 3) the divine pathways that are revealed to you along your journey. Once you have done the work to get clearer on who you are and who you are not, the next step is to get clear on what real vision is and what it is not. There are so many misconceptions about vision. Here is what you need to know as you move towards your real vision.

Real Vision Is...

Real Vision is transformational. As you learn more about yourself and show up to live out your values, it will invigorate you. When you level up and lead, you transform; you change and so does the world around you. Walking in alignment with your vision creates room for you to expand and make progress. It creates the opportunity for you to mature. At its essence, vision is less about the things you want to acquire and more about your values and how you want to show up in the world for yourself and others. There are seasons when you will grow, seasons when you will change, and seasons when you will share your gifts with those you have been called to serve. I refer to these transformative seasons as the season of the tree, the season of the butterfly, and the season of the sun. More on this later.

Real Vision is a Lifetime. Truly, a vision is a lifetime invitation to show up fully present, ready to love, and ready to lead; ready to use your gifts, skills, talents, and abilities as the opportunity presents itself. It is not a single goal. It isn't a simple three-step plan that you can work out over a month or even a single year. Annual and monthly goals are measuring tactics and accountability tools that keep you on task towards your real vision, but we are talking about a lifetime! While goals encompass aspects of your vision, they are only one part. Release any expectations that things will work out exactly as you have said; vision is about many things coming to fruition over a lifetime. You've heard the expression, "Speak what you seek until you see what you've said." Facts! But, what do you think will have to happen next once you see what you've said? A new aspect of the vision will emerge. Life continues after your goal is fulfilled. Congratulations! You have reached a new level and an expanded vision is required. This will happen many times over the course of your life.

Real Vision is Intentional. You must show up and create space to expand your vision. Not that you have to repeat the exact same actions every day, but the habit of making intentional space to tend to your vision is important. It is easy to get wrapped up in the daily demands of life and the responsibilities of your roles no matter what they are: employee, business owner, mom, wife, church member, sorority sister. These are important parts of your life. But these roles change over time, and you need to know who you are apart from those roles.

The benefits of making vision intentional and incorporating it into your daily life are:

- Helps you to check in regularly to maintain space for such changes.
- Allows you to take time for self-discovery which helps you to make <u>space</u> for your vision.

- Steadies your focus on faith and prayer for the endurance, patience, and discipline, which will keep your action-habits aligned with your vision.

Real Vision Ain't

Real Vision is not a vision board. Over the last twenty years, vision boards have increased in popularity with the invention of the vision board party. However, the focus routinely is on the party aspect of the event more than the vision. I love vision boards, and I even have vision board workshops every year. They can be a powerful tool in helping you articulate your vision, but your vision goes beyond the board. Otherwise, it is just a collage. But have no fear! Solutions are here. In chapter 14, I explain the ways you can make your vision board more authentic and meaningful to your life.

Real Vision isn't seeing everything. It is natural to be curious, to want to "see" everything. You don't have to see the entire staircase to walk up the stairs. You just need to see one step at a time to work your way forward. "But Alexandria, why would I walk up the stairs when there is an elevator?" Okay, girl, I hear you. Well, think about this. You don't need to see the inside of an elevator shaft in order to use an elevator. You see the doors open, you step in, and then wait until you see the doors open again. You see what you need to see, and you have faith and trust in what you do not. Vision is about nurturing the aspects of your desired life that have been revealed to you and illuminating that as much as possible so that the picture becomes clearer.

You invest in your future with what you choose to do today. Those possibilities increase based on your actions. Take the vision that you have right now, however big or small you think it might be, and nurture that. Water that. Let that seed grow into a forest of dreams that turns into reality. Your future is filled with things seen and unseen; outcomes that you can imagine and some that you never thought possible. They all exist already. Whether you can see them all or not is irrelevant. It is not your job. It is not your work. Do your work.

Real Vision is not the perfect circumstances. Adversity is not a sign of insignificance or lack of vision. Even if you feel like you're failing, you still matter. It's important to be mindful of things that will disengage you from your commitment to realize your vision.

One day while I was feeling particularly crappy about the excruciatingly slow progress I was making on a project, I thought, *Why do I keep screwing this up? I feel like a failure.* Automatically, without really thinking about it, I said aloud, "Because you are a failure." It was almost like another person said it. In the past, I would have been done for the rest of the day. I would've closed the laptop, went back to bed at three o'clock in the afternoon, not to be seen again until the morrow. In other words, throw the whole day away! However, as I have grown, I learned to guard myself against falling into criticism and negative self-talk that doesn't allow me to thrive. I have learned to call out the lies that people tell me and even the ones that I tell myself. I audibly responded to this negative thought. I said, "No, I am not a failure. I am human. I can make a mistake without being a mistake."

Immediately, I felt a sense of relief from capturing that thought and replacing it with truth. Even though I struggled that day to gain the momentum I desired, I kept going. I made progress because of my purpose. Since I am on purpose, I am not a mistake. God uses everything. The seasons that you sow, are just as important as the seasons you reap.

I have learned to accept that what appears to be a problem in my life, could very well just be the divine timing designed to mature me through the experience. Don't avoid the difficulties. Address areas of your life that are only designed to steal your time, energy, and joy. Negative self-talk, limiting beliefs, time wasters, and paralyzing perfectionism are some challenges you will need to address along this journey.

Real Vision isn't dishonest. Vision is rooted in values because it is meant for the greater good of a person, place, or community of people. Your vision cannot be to lie cheat, steal, or intentionally seek to do harm. In an attempt to fulfill a "vision" of being wealthy, if a person goes out and robs a bank, they have accomplished a crime, not a vision. Integrity and honesty matter when it comes to vision. You don't have to tear others down in order to build yourself up.

Real Vision ain't therapy. During a difficult season of grief, my experience led to mental and emotional stress, fatigue, and anxiety. Thankfully, I had access to several tools that ushered in my healing and strength including prayer; talking candidly to a small group of trusted friends; power-walking outdoors; seeking wise Godly counsel from my elders; decreasing or eliminating contact with toxic relationships; writing poetry; journaling; and making inspirational vision boards, and yes going to a licensed therapist. This combination of tools helped me heal and revealed the possibilities in my heart that have brought me a mighty long way. Visioning and vision boards can be positive, even cathartic experiences but are not a replacement for seeking professional support. If you are struggling with severe depression, suicidal thoughts, anxiety, addiction, or ongoing abuse, I want you to know that you are seen, your life is meaningful, and you are loved. You are worthy of God's love. Books like this are an excellent secondary source of encouragement and inspiration. However dear friend, it's not a substitute for primary sources of support which must be a priority. Don't let fear, shame, or stigma keep you from getting the help you need to live a full and healthy life. Although the events I share in this book happened many years ago, I still receive counseling, which gives me a safe space to check in and reminds me that I am not alone. I want you to have that same safe space to process so you can rise, thrive, and shine.

Reality Check Your Vision: Now it's time for you to define Real Vision for yourself! Which "Real Vision Is" principle will you embrace? Which "Real Vision Ain't" principle will you expel?

Chapter 4

IN SEARCH OF REAL VISION

"Your vision will become clear only when you look into your heart. Who looks outside dreams. Who looks inside awakens." Carl Jung

I have been asked, "Alexandria, why is it so important for you to help others walk in their vision?" Because there was a time I completely lost sight of who I was and who God created me to be. It wasn't just that I didn't have clarity around my vision. I was just flat out blind because I couldn't see much of anything. In my limited view, I had two goals in life: graduate from college and get married. Dassit! Beyond that, anything else I could see, I didn't believe could be real in my life like poetry, singing, writing, performing. These were minor footnotes at the time. Nothing important. Nothing to focus on or develop. I was quick to settle for regular. Mediocre. To me, it was just a mirage of an oasis in the desert. When I looked in the mirror, I didn't see a creative and confident young woman staring back at me. All I saw was inadequacy, insecurity, and an inability to be brave. The fear of honoring my gifts and walking in my vision outweighed the pursuit of an authentic life. I was a prisoner of my limitations, holding myself hostage, in an artificial experience.

In *Their Eyes Were Watching God*, Zora Neal Hurston writes, "There are years that ask questions, and years that answer." Well, after a few years of screaming into the void, demanding and downright begging God to hear me, I finally got the answers I needed, but they weren't the answers I was looking for.

Before then, my life was not defined by a real vision. It was defined by conditional love and the approval of others: my fiancé, my friends, my family, and my employer. Instead of being self-aware, I was completely unaware of me and overwhelmingly aware of what others liked or did not like about me. Earning approval and acceptance was constantly on my mind. I was consumed with doing everything right so that it would make people love and appreciate me.

I went from being a fun-loving people person to a self-hating people pleaser. There is a difference; but at that time, being a people person and a people pleaser were the same thing to me. I was all kinds of wrong. A people person has a vision to thrive and be interconnected with her community. A people pleaser also has a vision; however, it is not sustainable because it is almost completely focused on accomplishing tasks that are external. Everything is being poured out. Nothing is being poured in. The people pleaser's vision includes making people in her surroundings happy, even if it is at her own expense. It may sound awful, but in our society, women are often applauded for operating this way. Picture her. She helps everyone. She always says yes. She is lauded as a hero in her circle because she stops what she is doing, no matter what, and is always available to help. She goes above and beyond never asking or expecting anything else in return. Can you see her? Do you know her? Are you her? I could see this woman very well as she was staring at me in the mirror. But there was an ugly shadow to that reflection.

Perhaps the other side that is not discussed is this woman also has a hard time setting boundaries and saying no for fear of disappointing others, feeling guilty like she did something wrong. In her own life, she is in charge of all the things. Since she is so darn good at helping others, people keep on asking for her help. And you guessed it; she keeps saying yes, taking on the responsibility of other people's things. As a result, she tries unsuccessfully to control it, to manage expectations and outcomes. She can be pretty successful at this whole taking care of other people's stuff. But her own life is neglected and mismanaged. It seems like she can get everyone else together except for herself. She is ashamed to ask for help to get her own needs met because she feels she can't ask. Besides, she is the one others rely on to get their needs met. As a result, she suffers in silence. She is willing to set herself on fire just to keep everyone else warm. Been there, done that, and I have the burnt t-shirt to prove it.

Trust me when I tell you that it was not the way, the truth, or the light because I am not Jesus, and it wasn't my job to be running around trying to save people. However, internal pressure and external expectations led me to think that this was what I was supposed to do. It was just how life worked. I considered it not only normal but necessary. I thought, *This is how every woman gets to her happily ever after. Be who they need you to be. Help them and they will love you. And at some point, you will carve out a little space for yourself along the way. That's just the way it is.*

I didn't see the writing on the wall that read, "Sis, you in danger girl!" Insert Whoopi Goldberg meme from the movie *Ghost* here. Even if I had seen it, I'm not sure if I would have paid attention to it. I might have ignored the sign and walked right on by. Have you ever ignored the warning signs in your life? Did you miss the bright red flags on a friendship or relationship? Have you ever just looked up one day and realized that you are showing up in the world completely opposite of the vision you have for your life? I know I did. It would be a long time before I learned just how far off my own path I was. Sadly, the vision I had for my life had almost nothing to do with who God created me to be.

Then one day, my life came screeching to a halt. My wedding was cancelled with no plans to postpone or reschedule. The contract for my job was about to be over and I was informed that it would not be renewed. As if that weren't enough for my little plate of life, I was involved in a shooting on my way to church one Sunday morning in the car with a friend from college. Coming from where I'm from in Los Angeles, California the sound of gunfire was very common to me. It was as regular as the sound of a helicopter flying in the night sky. In my old neighborhood, it is considered a tool of survival to distinguish how far away the shots are, what direction they are coming from, and if they are moving closer or further away just by the echo of the sound of a bullet leaving the barrel. In just a few seconds, you need to determine if it is time to duck, run, or shelter in place. There are colors you don't wear and places you don't go. This is how one determines if you are safe.

From the time between the first and second shots, I knew we were not safe. The sound was close, and the shots kept coming. "They" shot out my friend's front window as we sped away from the sound of bullets ricocheting off the outside of her car, heads down, too scared to lift up or see where we were going, steering the car back to my parent's house just three blocks away. "They" continued shooting at us. I remember praying that there were no pedestrians in the street. No children out to play. We honked the horn as a warning to get out of the way. It wasn't safe. The police identified three bullet holes and extracted one bullet that was still lodged in her car. The police took our report. The officers were polite and came within 30 minutes of our call. But ultimately, the officers explained that there was very little they could do since no one had been shot. We should be so grateful, the officers explained. I was beginning to have a panic attack, the first one that I can ever recall, so I don't know what else they said. I never found out who "They" were. Just another day living in the 'hood. Just another day around the way. The hood was home. I loved my neighbors who were like family, the culture, the food, and the loving connection in my community. There was so much of that. But it stood in stark contrast to the violence. It was one thing to grow up around the elements; it was another to be in them. It was a moment that critically altered my life.

For months after, I isolated myself in my dorm room and the office on campus at my university where I worked. My emotional, financial, and physical safety had all been threatened at the same time. Yet, there was more to come. I didn't share this with anyone at the time, but I almost dropped out of college even though it was my senior year. To be honest, I nearly failed. I didn't want to be outside because of all that I had recently gone through. Instead of taking the campus shuttle back and forth to school, I waited hours for my friend and co-worker Patrice to get out of class and give me a ride every day. I did not want to attend class. She and other co-workers went to get my lunch for me. I didn't want to go back home and visit my family on weekends like I usually did. I did not want to go to church. I did not want to leave my apartment. Before I knew it, weeks had gone by and professors were contacting me, asking why I hadn't been in class and where were all of my assignments? It was nearly graduation and, before this, I was a good student. What was happening? Inquiring minds wanted to know. Internally, I felt like I was drowning, and the world was on fire. But I was too ashamed to tell them. "Just under a lot of stress" was my reply. So, I just asked for packets of make-up assignments to earn a passing grade.

This was a fine solution for all but one class. It was a graduation requirement; a one-unit freshmen course that I'd put off until senior year. I failed it. No amount of make-up work or explaining what happened could make this right. In fact, the professor didn't even believe my Tales From the Hood episode 3- "Girl Shot At On the Way to Church" thing. He actually rolled his eyes and held up his hand to stop me by saying "Well whatever happened, you didn't complete the assignments, and I can't give you a grade that you didn't earn." That was a low blow for me, pressing into every unworthy angst that a black girl from the hood on financial aid, working two jobs while going to school full-time and still pulling a 3.0 GPA could have. I put all my pride aside and practically begged, graveled for an Incomplete so that I could finish the course over the summer. The answer was still no. I asked again. My final appeal was rejected and dismissed by the department chair the week of graduation. The decision had been made.

No such accommodations would be granted. I failed the class. I was allowed to walk in cap and gown. I was allowed to give my graduation speech during the ceremony as planned. But I was not allowed to graduate.

Dear Langston Hughes, did you ever find out exactly what happens to a dream deferred? Like a shriveled-up grape turned raisin in the sun, I oscillated somewhere between dragging the heavy load and about to explode. I had all the feels. Shame. Guilt. Anger. Pisstivity of the highest degree. But no college degree. It felt like proof that I wasn't "good enough." Exhibit A that I should NOT dare to dream bigger because even my little mediocre vision of graduating and getting married was already too much to ask for, right? Imposter syndrome was agonizing. Here I was, robed in cap and gown, trying not to break down and cry as we marched in. Come on! I was giving the graduation speech and just found out I wasn't actually graduating for crying out loud. I felt like a complete and utter failure. All my hopes and dreams gone down the drain. I failed my professors. I failed my mentors. I failed my family. I failed my fiancé... ehh ex-fiancé. I failed myself. Cue the violins, the orchestra, and the band because they were all set to play at my pity party. To make matters worse, most of the people who I'd spent so much time trying to please were not even there to help me through it. Ouch. I had been the "good girl" but still, why didn't I feel loved? It was then that I understood that love is not a reward for good behavior. After years of these conditional exchanges, especially in friendships just as much as my romantic relationships, I saw how playing small in order to fit into someone else's life led me to play small in every aspect of my life. I simultaneously had an abundance of problems and a complete lack of confidence, clarity, or support. Broken and discouraged, I grew tired of searching for the light at the end of the tunnel. I couldn't see a thing. My eyes couldn't see anything except tears.

Reality Check Your Vision: After a season of brokenness, what do you need in order to heal and refocus so you can get the blessing and the lesson? Has hardship in your personal life affected your professional or educational goals?

Chapter 5

BROKEN VISION

"Heartbreak opens onto the sunrise

For even breaking is opening

And I am broken

I'm open…Open to the possibilities within."

– Dee Rees[iii]

Before you get clear on your vision, you need to get clear on who you are. After experiencing so much heartbreak and incurring the debt for a wedding that did not happen, I was broke, and broken. Add to that multiple funerals of dear loved ones in a short period of time and I had become undone. I was exhausted and numb from grieving. And it wasn't just the funerals. It was everything. I was in spiritual disarray and mad at God. I had insomnia for months and extreme stress that led to anxiety. I became weak and malnourished from the loss of appetite. My skin broke out, and my eczema flared up. The migraine headaches I experienced as a child came back. I was miserable.

"Wow, you look great! Losing weight and getting healthy I see. Good for you!" I ran into a friend from college who was referring to the fifteen pounds of weight I'd lost since she'd seen me last. I wanted to scream, *But can't you see? I'm falling apart!* I was the unhealthiest I had ever been. But instead, I just blinked back the tears, put on a half-smile, and politely ended the conversation as quickly as possible. Who had I become?

I Need A Break. Life had broken me down in all the ways that mattered to me – spiritually, financially, and relationally. Defining myself by the standards of others for so long impacted every aspect of my life. I was so stressed, fatigued, and malnourished that I became physically sick, in desperate need of healing. All of the visions that I had for my life were quickly fading. I didn't realize just yet that they were illusions, so I didn't respond too well when it all began to slip away.

At first, I held on tight to my old way of life even though I knew it wasn't the right thing for me. For a minute, I actually went back to dating my ex-fiancé, trying to "make things work." In reality, I just didn't know what was next for me. I set out to try to improve a bad situation and work things out. *Maybe I haven't tried hard enough, prayed long enough, compromised enough,* I thought. Of course, these were all lies from, as my grandmother Nora would say, "The very pit of hell." I tried anyway. But that only made things worse. Instead of moving forward to see what God had for me, I ran back into the burning building I'd been rescued from. Instead of moving forward to see what God was trying to show me, I ran from the process of getting to know who I'd been created to be; without a degree, without a wedding ring, and without a plan for my career. I carried on, trying to fix things that I didn't break. Instead of communication and compromise, I was flat out settling. It wasn't a good look. I wonder if God was like, "Child, what are you doing?" I couldn't hold on any further. I hit rock bottom with a loud thump.

From Breakdown to Breakthrough. Once I was there, quiet and alone, I had an epiphany of sorts. I closed my eyes and imagined myself broke and broken, constantly striving to do the right thing and please the right people, constantly disappointed in myself, fighting for my place in the world. But here in this place, none of that mattered. I felt like I had lost everything and had nothing left. But that was the epiphany. There was nothing left hovering over me. No one to please. No one to determine who I was supposed to be from that day forward. No one to stress me the heck out. I felt a sense of relief and a sense of self. Now, it was just up to me to pray and decide which pieces of my life were my own, pick them up, and keep moving forward.

This breakdown led me to a breakthrough. I was broken, but perhaps I was just broken open. There is a process in Japanese pottery called Kintsukuroi which means "golden repair." This is a process where broken pieces of pottery are repaired and sealed back together with gold or silver, making the final version of the vessel even more beautiful because it has been broken. This is the best way to describe what I felt was happening to me. It makes me think of a gospel song, "The Potter's House," by Tramaine Hawkins based on Jeremiah 17 and 18.

"In case you have fallen by the wayside of life, dreams and visions shattered, you're all broken inside. You don't have to stay in the shape that you're in. The Potter wants to put you back together again." Every day, I felt less like I was broken and more like the shackles in my life had been broken. Each time I strengthened my boundaries and listened to what my body and spirit needed, I felt more and more free to be authentically me.[iv]

As I sought to pick up the pieces of my life, I did three (3) things that changed the way I lived:

1. **A Fresh Awareness.** I no longer accepted the path to a dead end. During this transformation, I began the long journey of seeing myself differently. A fresh awareness came over me. It was the ever so small possibility that all was not lost, and this was where I needed to be. I needed proof that this process had a purpose. I had a hard time wrapping my mind around it being a "good thing," because nothing felt good about it. But it was in fact a good thing and so much more. It was a "God thing." It was like taking a sobering dose of medicine with the chalky aftertaste. Just like medicine, some things can be good for you without feeling good to you. This was my medicine. As I began healing, I saw how my old ways of seeing, my old ways of being, were damaging as I examined them up close and personal. This transformation allowed me to grow. I was different. In this season, I was acquiring a new vision for my life.

2. **A Renewal.** During the most difficult times, as I continued to spiral, I knew it was necessary to make some changes in my heart in order to make progress in other areas of my life. As a

Christian, I saw how my spiritual life was in disarray. My relationship with Jesus needed some serious repair. The things that Jesus proclaimed in the Gospels of grace, love, redemption, peace, and hope were exactly what I needed to move forward. One important choice was to recommit to my faith in Jesus Christ like never before. My life could only be defined by the Creator. My being was already set. I didn't have to convince others to give me love and acceptance. I already had it from Christ who freely loved me, who accepted all of me, and who saw me for who I really am. I already had it from those who generously shared their gifts with me and I with them. I didn't have to fight for my place in the world. It was already mine. I just had to accept that, keep showing up to see what was possible, and what was next. God showed me how desperate I was for acceptance that I was ready to give up who I was created to be in order to become what others wanted me to be. But what would it profit me to gain that acceptance from the world and lose my soul? God's plan was better. I committed to never lose sight of the worthy and loved person I was created to be.

3. **A Choice.** I made the choice to begin again. I realized that I needed to start over and rebuild my life; but this time with a strong foundation. I needed to start with a stronger sense of self and a more focused vision for the person that existed within. I was done letting "failure" or rejection define me. I was done being the person who hid from the world and lived her life through the vision of others. No matter who stayed in my life or left, they did not make me, nor could they break me. It was then that I realized my vision mattered. And my vision mattered because I mattered. Until this point, I'd missed the memo

on that. God said it. That settles it. So, I am passing the note on to you. You matter!

4. **A Voice.** My ability to embrace choice in my life allowed me to use that to strengthen my voice. From an early age, I loved education. Learning was fun to me. But after all that had transpired, I'd begun to hate school. I even considered trying to buck the system and pretend that I didn't even need that little one unit for my degree. I could apply for jobs and no one would know. But I would know, and it wouldn't be authentic. After thinking long and hard about it, I couldn't let this difficult situation leave such a bad taste in my mouth that it kept me away from my vision and my voice as a scholar. I finally re-enrolled in school to finish my degree. In addition to taking the one class over that I needed to make my graduation official, which I passed, I took additional courses to prepare me for graduate school. In these courses, I truly found a new layer of freedom. Since these were not courses required for my graduation, I was utterly unbothered about the outcome and the grade. I engaged in class in a completely different way. I chose topics that peeked my academic curiosity rather than topics I thought might earn an A from the professor. Somehow, I still got an A. It blew my mind. You mean I could raise my voice, respectfully disagree with the professor, use creative as well as critical thinking skills and still thrive? It was on like never before. There was no turning back. That year that I had deemed evil turned out to be purely for my good. I traveled the country on scholarships and fellowships granted by professors at my university so that I could present on panels at prestigious conferences. I published more papers and poetry that year than I ever had in the past. I found my voice to get on stage and perform poetry again, something that had been discouraged in previous

relationships. To the surprise of some, I turned off my autoresponder, my automatic "sure, ok," to nearly every request, and I found the voice to say no with confidence. Equally as important, I found the freedom in my voice to say an authentic and enthusiastic yes without any regrets!

Reality Check Your Vision: Reflect on your life's journey: what is one experience you can recall where you felt like everything went opposite of your plans and you thought it was permanently broken but later realized that there was an important lesson in the experience?

Chapter 6

YOUR VISION MATTERS

"There is freedom waiting for you,
On the breezes of the sky,
And you ask, 'What if I fall?'
Oh, but my darling,
What if you fly?"
-Erin Hanson, Untitled[v]

The vision that began to emerge came from my values and core beliefs once I was able to chip away at the rust and erosion. That came from me trying to determine what it looked like to show up whole in the world. And that was the best thing possible for me. Beyond that, I didn't have an actual plan for my future. I was just learning to stand still in the present moment. Making plans for the future was a distant goal. This reality at first made me feel helpless. But soon, I was able to emerge as a refreshed woman with renewed passion and purpose. Had my vision began with goals, objectives, and accomplishments, I could have easily slid right back into striving, performing, and trying to look like a good person on the outside rather than being a good person on the inside. Even now, years later, I still have to check my core to maintain a balance between doing and being. I discovered that the more I took time to detox and remove negativity from my life, the more I craved a healthier, more authentic way of operating. The more I took a journey of self-discovery, the more clearly I could see all these amazing things God placed in me that had been there all along. Through prayer and support from faith-filled women, the Holy Spirit began to show me who I really was, and as I healed, I began to see the possibilities of this growth. I began to see who I could become and how I could positively impact others.

Once I did realize it, I ran with this newfound understanding. Aligning my values with my vision was an important part of that. As a result, I had to spend some time shedding old ways of doing and thinking to become a woman who accepted nothing less than God's best. I was in desperate need of a joyful, hopeful, love filled life. I restarted the process of getting to know love, God, and myself again.

From the time I was born, my grandmother, known affectionately as Sugar-dew or "Shoodoo," cast a vision for me. Her goal was for me to read every day as a child and grow up to pursue higher education and receive a college degree that she was not able to receive in her youth. In her lifetime, I received two. And she was ever so proud to take the Greyhound bus across the country (yep two to three-day trips as she refused to fly) to attend any graduation where her grandchildren walked across the stage in cap and gown. But her vision for my life, beyond getting a degree, was that my grandmother wanted me to be a woman who was knowledgeable of the world so that I could have choices in my life. She did not want me to be limited by what I was told, as many women in her generation were, especially Black women in Alabama where she was from. Throughout my childhood, she always saved newspaper and magazine clippings that she felt would inspire me. I was gifted with this collection of clippings, in a box, on my high school graduation day. It was a treasure trove of reminders about what it means to hold vision. She'd held this vision for me since I was a child. I poured over the love letters and special notes she had given to me over the years. It helped me remember what I came from and what I was capable of becoming.

I also began journaling, a practice that my mother Jeanette had long instilled in me and my sisters since elementary school. Learning did not stop in the classroom she would say. So, every day after summer camp, my sister and I had to sit down with our red journals and write about our day. I called on that childhood practice to help me to reorient myself and reimagine my life. Originally, I hated journaling. I preferred poetry and short stories. But in the blind visionless season I was in, my creative muscle had been weakened. Besides, I realized that I needed to dig deeper into my reality rather than hide in characters or iambic pentameter. From these musings of my mother and grandmother, I began making collages of words and images that inspired me. They gave me another way to speak my hopes and dreams. This is the origin story of vision boards in my life. It included words and personal pictures as well as images from magazines. It included journaling past It was simple and powerful. Every time I looked at it, I smiled and was reminded of the beauty that is possible.

What a difference a year can make. As you grow, the days are long, but the years are short. Within a year or two, my life was completely different. I received new job opportunities that were not visible to me before. I graduated and obtained my degree. I co-authored and published projects I never thought possible. I was invited as a guest speaker to colleges and youth groups across the country. I dared myself to perform poetry on stage at one of the most culturally rich art scenes in Los Angeles. I was able to nurture new friendships and set new boundaries in existing ones. I traveled more and eventually moved across the country from Los Angeles to Washington D.C. for a career changing opportunity. I met Presidential Candidate Barack Obama and a host of other political and cultural organizers who I still have the pleasure of knowing today. I eventually returned to school to get a master's degree on a teaching fellowship (similar to a scholarship). There were quite a few people who didn't like this new me, including some family. It wasn't easy, but it was necessary. Year after year, I healed from the pain of the past and turned it into the fuel that powered my vision.

The Situation Room. However, there was one area that I did not grow quickly in at all. Your challenges may not be the same as mine, but there may be areas where it takes more time to cultivate this new foundation needed to move forward. Since this book is about authentic vision, it is important for me to keep it real with you. During those first few years of exponential growth, I felt like a light bulb was turned on with a renewed sense of self. Yet, my renewed self was jumping in and out of un-renewed, unenlightened, random situationships. A lot of them.

A situationship is when two people look like a relationship, talk like a relationship, walk like a relationship, plan the future together like a relationship but, you guessed it, are NOT in an actual relationship.

If situationships had a sound, it would be nails on a chalk board. If it had a look, it would be the original Gordon Gartrelle shirt Denise Huxtable made for Theo. If it had a smell, it would be the fragrant scent of hot garbage set on fire in the middle of a hot, ninety-degree, August day with 30% humidity burning outside your front door. You see where I am going with this. In other words, this ain't what you want.

I left behind the bad relationship, but I did not leave behind the bad habits or the bad attitude that I developed in that relationship. I walked away with all sorts of unmanaged expectations about life and love. I took all of that baggage with me. It only served to cloud my vision as I moved forward. My relationship status changed, but I had not yet changed. Sis, it was a process.

Relationship is the area in my life that taught me that knowing what I don't want is not the same as knowing what I do want. And knowing what I want is not the same as knowing what I need. That truth changed everything for me. Now that I'd changed, I still needed to grow. Even when I did take more time to expand my vision of a healthy, committed, and faith-centered relationship, I continued to date people who did not share this vision. It was a steep learning curve.

Out of these often-confusing situations, I did gain some clarity about what I wanted from a relationship and how I needed to walk in my vision to get there. As a result, I learned early on not to volunteer my heart as tribute. What once took me three months to figure out, I was gradually able to see in three dates. Progress. But overall, my dating choices did not align with the vision God began to reveal in my life. He showed me that love changes things, and that choosing the right partner could have a tremendous impact on my life. As I opened my heart, I began to see a vision for deep abiding love in a relationship that gave me chills. Commitment. Authentic communication. Quality time. Travel. Relationship retreats. Marriage ministry. Breaking generational cycles. Reading books together. Building businesses. Serving the community. Leaving a legacy. Leading together. Imagine having this profound revelation while you are dating Random Guy #12 who is not even sure if he wants to get married and is already trying to debate me about a woman's place. All I could say back then was, "Dear God, why am I still single?!" That's another story for another time. However, I share this now to say that this season did serve a great purpose.

When it came to dating, my actions were out of alignment with my vision and my values. Dating taught me a valuable lesson about vision. You can gain the clarity. You can do the spiritual and personal development workshops. You can even read all the books and actually get clear about your values. But if you don't do the work of walking in your vision, implementing what you have learned, and aligning your actions to what you believe, it will not add up. Your reality will remain disconnected and disjointed from your vision.

I was single for six years before I met my husband. Being single also meant that I was discovering my personal vision in the area of relationships rather than being an echo chamber from a man to get his approval and affections. God had to deliver me from wanting a relationship so badly that I was willing to be like the would-be princess of Zumunda in *Coming to America*: "Whatever you like." I had to realize that my vision mattered. Honestly, I needed every single day of that lengthy process to arrive at the place where I was able to live out my vision and values in a healthy relationship; where I was able to freely give and receive love with confidence and joy the way it was intended to be experienced.

By the time my husband and I began our relationship, I was abundantly clear on what I was and was not 'finna do. Yes, I said not 'finna, a linguistically colloquial phrase for refuse, decline, or discontinue. I was not 'finna settle, chase, tolerate or accept an unloving relationship in an effort to arrive at the destination of marriage. I had standards in dating before, but this time was different. This time, it was no longer about me judging the men I dated to figure out if he was "the one." This time, it was about disciplining myself and staying true to my values. I was the one who needed to strengthen my voice, to let my yes be yes and my no be no. I was the one who was in a covenant relationship with God. It became an opportunity for me to live authentically and true to my vision, no matter my relationship status. I learned to honor me, as a woman baring the fingerprint of God, whole and complete, with or without a husband and family. I required of myself that the only relationship I could fully open my heart to must be holistically rooted in three (3) areas: Agape (God), Philos (kinship/family), and Eros (romantic). Until that time came, I walked alone. As usual, God was right. Choosing a life partner, getting married, and entering a covenant union has had a tremendous impact on my life. It has had it's share of ups and downs, but it has been worth the journey.

I shared this story with you so that you can see that while I experienced rapid recovery and transformation in some areas of my life, there were other areas that moved as slow as molasses rolling up hill. Relationships became the battle ground to show me how important it is to stay true to who you are, even when your reality does not reflect your vision yet. Those years of singleness tested every belief I had about love, worthiness, compatibility, marriage, and faith. I am glad I took the journey to dig deeper into my beliefs, values, and vision. This allowed me to see clearly when the right man finally did come along who wanted to create a shared vision with me.

The years of consistent spiritual growth and personal leadership development strengthened my resolve to remain steadfast in my values and committed to growing every day. Through this process, I was able to see myself clearly and differently than at any other time before. Through this process, God revealed all these hidden desires in my heart to become someone who I loved! Someone who created impact in the world, through training leaders, thinkers, public servants, and entrepreneurs. Someone creative and strategic. Someone like me.

I became fully aware that I matter. My vision matters. And it is also true of you. Getting clear on who you are is the first step, but sometimes that starts by getting clear on what you are not.

Reality Check Your Vision: Have you ever felt insignificant or unworthy? What person, experience, or idea has ever made you feel like you, your vision, or your life did not matter? What do you do to combat this lie and stand in your courage?

Chapter 7

THE MYTHS OF VISION PERFECTION

Real vision is not created in a vacuum of perfection.

#FreeYourRealVision

-Alexandria @YesSheLeads

"I think perfectionism is just fear in fancy shoes and a mink coat, pretending to be elegant when actually it's just terrified. Because underneath that shiny veneer, perfectionism is nothing more than a deep existential angst that says, again and again, 'I am not good enough....'"
— Elizabeth Gilbert, Big Magic: Creative Living Beyond Fear[vi]

R eal vision is not created in a vacuum of perfection. It is time to redefine what being perfect is really. It's time to embrace a more honest and functional look at vision in our messy and complicated world. When I finally began to understand what the author Elizabeth Gilbert was saying – that the pursuit of perfection is often driven by fear – I knew that this impacted so many areas of my thoughts and expectations. And of course, it shifted my perspective on vision. From this, I have come to embrace real vision over an idealized "perfect vision." A real vision is not without flaw; actually, it's the imperfections that make it accessible and more authentic. Instead of perfect, a real vision is perfected over time because it is consistently pursued and constantly maturing. Here are the seven (7) myths of vision perfection:

1-Perfect Vision. When you go to the doctor and take the eye exam, what is the number one thing you want the doctor to say? "Congratulations. You have perfect 20/20 Vision." By most standards, 20/20 vision is considered the best eyesight to have. It's perfect, right? Actually, 20/20 vision is defined as a measurement of "normal" sight by the American Optometric Association because it only measures the clarity that a person can see 20 feet in front of them. But does that mean the vision is perfect? There are other factors to consider for this designation such as peripheral vision, depth perception, and color vision. These are elements that change how "perfect vision" is defined. For example, a person can have 20/20 vision and be colorblind, which impairs what they see. They have the twenty-foot range of sight but can't see everything. Therefore, 20/20 vision does not actually describe perfect vision. Let that sink in.

The standard by which our culture measures perfect vision isn't perfect at all. It is important for a visionary like you to understand this because the idea of 20/20 vision tends to put vision up on a pedestal of flawless perfection. Trying to achieve this perfect idea can quickly lead to feelings of inadequacy when things don't work out perfectly. Break free from this notion in order to unpack an empowering definition of vision for your life.

2-Perfect Sight. Vision is not the same as sight. There are ways that having vision and eyesight are similar. In both vision and sight, you take a close look at what is around you to provide information. However, there are many places where vision and sight differ. For many, the loss of eyesight is degenerative, meaning as a person gets older and the more their sight is used, it becomes weaker and things become less clear. With vision, there is a stark difference. The more you use your vision over time, the clearer it gets. Sight is about what you can literally see. Vision is about what you can visualize, feel, think, anticipate, and desire for yourself, as well as your community, which is not always apparent to the naked eye. Vision is also comprised of what has been divinely revealed to you through other types of sight: foresight, insight, and hindsight.

3-Perfect Predictions. Vision is often approached as what you can see clearly so that you can make a prediction about what is next. But a clear vision doesn't mean you can perfectly predict what will and won't happen because vision isn't an exact roadmap. It's more like a compass to help you move in the right direction.

If a child picks up a Doc McStuffins toy stethoscope and says, "Mommy, I want to be a doctor," the parent says, "Then you will become a doctor. When you grow up, you can be anything you want to be." Such sweet encouragement will empower that child to dream, imagine, and be inspired to expand her horizons. But is every parent really predicting the medical career of their child? Of course not. The parent is nurturing the child's vision that will continue to mature as she grows. What the parent is really saying is, "I want my child to know she can be anything she wants to be! I'm so glad she is already imagining herself doing important things." That is a vision the parent holds for their child. They will get older and outgrow many things on the way to pursuing new interests. Children are allowed to pivot, to change. And so are you, even when obstacles seem to stand in the way.

You have to allow, and dare I say invite, flexibility into your life in order for your vision to transform. An experience with my youngest sister, Diamond, is a great example. She wanted to be a veterinarian as a little girl because she loved dogs. By junior high, she wanted to be a medical doctor, so my parents enrolled her in a medical preparatory program for urban high school students in Los Angeles named after the genius physician Dr. Charles Drew, the inventor of blood bank storage and the first director of the Red Cross. While other teenagers hung out at the local Burger King after school, my sister was shadowing medical professionals doing rounds at a local hospital. It was there she learned that she didn't want to be a doctor but really wanted to be a gynecological nurse specializing in postpartum and neo-natal deliveries. This was really exciting for her, but I wasn't the most encouraging person in the mix. She was seventeen, and I was the older "grown" sister so of course I thought I knew better. "But you are going to be a doctor. A black woman doctor from the 'hood! You are going to change your mind about nursing because being a doctor is better." Ouch! I was so wrong. Sometimes, people you love will not always understand your growth. You see, I was frozen in time to the little girl ten years prior who said she wanted to be a doctor. She was transforming and expanding her vision on her path to personal purpose.

Children will play with different toys and, as they grow, they will imagine other careers. The same is true for you. Notice what inspires you; the things you are deeply drawn too. Imagine what that can look like for you. Use it for its intended purpose – inspiration and information. But give yourself permission to grow. You will age, change, and mature along the way. Don't freeze yourself in time where you feel stuck to a prediction made in the past.

4-Perfect Pillars of Support. Have you ever had a vision that was so profoundly clear to you but your loved ones didn't support it? It is a story shared by many on their journey towards the real vision. In this situation, I think of the Wilbur and Orville Wright, also known as the Wright Brothers. These two First Generation Americans, PK's aka preacher's kids, who did not even finish high school, literally invented the world's first airplane. They successfully did what great engineers and aeronautical experts tried to do for decades. You might think everyone who knew them was rooting for their success. Not true. Their father, an important Bishop in his church, was not very supportive of their endeavors at all. Before they achieved flight, it is reported that their father actually encouraged the brothers to stop this pursuit and take another career path. He once famously said, "Flying is reserved for the angels." How would you feel if you were walking in your vision and doing something that could change lives forever, but you were discouraged from continuing? Would you give up? Well, the Wright Brothers didn't, and today you travel around the world on planes because of the technology they created over 100 years ago.

The question that remains is why? Why do people that you respect and love, or those who may even want the best for you, not always support the vision you have? It is speculated that Bishop Milton Wright, the father of the Wright Brothers, wanted his sons to follow his steps into ministry. But that wasn't their path. Another popular theory is that Milton feared for his son's lives. After all, many of the forefathers of flight who came before the Wright Brothers died testing out their planes. Couple that with the fact that Milton lost his wife and other children to death and diseases of the times, it may have created a looming sense of grief over the family. As the patriarch of the family, it is reasonable that Milton had concern for his two sons. In your case, it may be reasonable that loved one's express concerns if your vision catches them off guard. However, those reasons cannot make your decisions. Your support is not coming from perfect people. They have their own journey, their own vision, and their own fears to contend with; you have yours. You must proceed with the actions that align with the vision in your heart. When people really love you, over time, they will come to see the joy and impact that walking in your vision brings. It's okay if they don't see it now. But, don't shrink down to fit into their idea of who you are. You just keep walking in alignment.

Yes, seek wise counsel. Yes, really listen to those you know genuinely care for you. Ultimately though, it is your vision, so don't quit because of the objections of others. Perhaps the Wright Brothers thrived because of their father's concerns. They still did what they felt called to do, but the measure of safety they experienced was much higher than average at that time. In fact, many of their predecessors died in experiments trying to create human flight. Add to that their father's concerns and that may have resulted in them taking extra precautions during those experiments hundreds of feet in the air. But they did not quit. Remember, it is YOUR vision. Everyone doesn't get the privilege of seeing what you see. The Wright Brothers had a vision to do the "impossible" and provide for their family. They were able to accomplish both.

When it came to my sister and my wavering support of her career as a nurse, her growth made me scared. The truth, the whole truth, and nothing but the truth is that I didn't know how to help her. My family made sure that we were exposed to all kinds of careers growing up, but medical examples were limited to shots at the doctor, Grey's Anatomy, and House. So, when my baby sister declared at age twelve, she wanted to be a medical doctor, I started researching programs and scholarships for students, especially for young girls who wanted careers in the S.T.E.M. field (science, technology, engineering, and math) because S.T.E.M. was in! Then and now, it is a male-dominated field with high-demand and high paying jobs. I felt prepared to be of assistance. But nursing? I had no clue. I started researching the nursing field to better see how I could support my sister. There were a few programs and even fewer scholarships in this field. After doing more research, I learned that although the number of people entering the nursing field was down from previous years, there wasn't a huge effort to recruit millennials or Gen Z students into the field. Unlike the prestige of S.T.E.M., it was considered women's work and, on top of that, it was considered less valuable because it was a trade. Yet, many women, especially Black and Latino women, have built esteemed careers in nursing, supporting their parents and children along the way. Can you believe it? They were devaluing skills that any doctor would agree they cannot function without; yet, being a nurse was less important because it was women's work. They help to save lives. They are essential workers. They make a difference in the world. They are women with vision. And here I was doing the same thing. I was diminishing the value of this field when I should have been supporting it.

After this reality check, I told my sister she could be anything she wanted to be, just as when she was twelve years old, and I committed to help her as much as I could along the way. I assured her the work that she valued, the work that is incredibly important in the medical field, was important to me too. She expressed interest. She was nurtured and supported as her vision matured. She brought her community along with her. I learned from her just as she learned in school. And now she has a degree in health science, has launched a career working in one of the largest hospitals in California, and is pursuing her RN (registered nurse) certification.

It is not your job to convince anyone of your vision. Don't allow the fears of others to stop you from pursuing your vision. Allow yourself the space to grow, and with that, your vision will grow also.

5-Perfect Path. Just as every child won't grow up to become a doctor, everything we see for ourselves won't materialize exactly as seen in magazines with perfectly poised images that vision boards draw inspiration from. You can create the most perfect vision board, but it doesn't mean you have a perfect path to your vision. The goal is inspiration, not imitation. You are the real thing. You are going to materialize a real-life success story, full of tests and a testimony. It will have high mountain tops and moments in the valley. You were made to do more than manifest a carbon copy of an artificial life from a magazine or a carefully curated selection of photos on "the gram." You are not your vision board. You are the real thing. You are a vision in progress.

Have you received exactly what you thought you wanted, only to find that it's not as fulfilling as you hoped it would be? Or my personal favorite, you see the opportunity so clearly that you just *know* it's yours. In fact, you can taste it, yet, it didn't quite work out. You don't know why, but you just didn't get it. And the "it" in your life can be anything: passed over for a promotion, the "perfect" relationship didn't work out, or you were outbid on the purchase of your dream home. Then down the line, the next month or year, you clearly see why it didn't work out. Here's the big surprise. You're happy about it! As a matter of fact, you thank God that it didn't work out the exact way you saw it. It is in that moment you realize it. You thought your vision was clear before, but you gained clarity on your way through it. Sometimes, you get the corner office, the money, or the man. And sometimes, you get the lesson that clears your pathway to new understanding. New growth. That growth will lead you to the clarity required for each season of your life.

6-Perfect Picture. A vision is not just one picture, one singular image of who you are supposed to become and what you plan to do. It is much more like mosaic – a combination of all these smaller images brought together to create one big picture. This is one reason why vision boards are such a popular representation of the visions people have for their lives. Because vision is long term, it spans the course of time, capturing major and minor milestones in your life that are building up to your expansive vision. This is not a linear process because you do not live a linear life. You may be tempted to get hung up here looking for an exact road map or a clear four-step process which doesn't exist. Let's shift the picture a bit. You may look at a Fortune 500 CEO who graduated from an Ivy League business school, interned at a great firm, landed the middle manager job, and worked her way up to CEO as the perfect picture of success. But remember, vision is divine, and everyone is fighting a battle you know nothing about. It is not just about wanting to prosper in success but your soul as well.

You cannot fear an "imperfect" or non-linear path. Your vision comes from God and rests in your spirit. God can use every part of your life to be a vehicle for your vision. Take NBA Legend Ervin "Magic" Johnson for example, a man who has literally had one career his entire life. I have so many special memories watching him play with my father, enjoying his finesse, his sportsmanship, and his success. As a young boy, Magic fell in love with the game, played all through high school, and got scholarships to college. He goes from college to the pro's and in his rookie year, he leads his team to a championship and is named the MVP – most valuable player. Then goes on to play basketball at the Olympics. When he retired from his successful career, he continued a career as a basketball sports commentator and a part owner of, you guessed it, a basketball league. It wouldn't be far-fetched for you to say that basketball is his life.

Except, he doesn't see it the same way. As a huge fan of Magic Johnson, I have listened to many interviews where he said that basketball was just the vehicle for him to live out his professional dreams, but it is not what is most important to him. As a man that overcame an HIV diagnosis in an era that meant it was a death sentence, Magic Johnson values things like his health, his family, and his financial legacy for generations of his family to come. This may sound a bit cliché, but he pivoted many times to redeem a family life and reputation that were nearly destroyed. Everyone does not exercise their vision and values to do the same when the picture isn't perfect. I'm sure you can think of an athlete or two that comes to mind who has neglected their physical or mental health; the athletes plastered on the news because they did not manage their finances to secure the bag for themselves, let alone the next generation; and those that publicly abuse or embarrass their families.

There is one thing I respect even more than Magic Johnson bringing home all those Laker championship trophies. With authenticity and transformation, he used his profile to raise awareness about testing for HIV and AIDS, particularly among men in Black and Brown communities. For many years, he became the public figure of people living with HIV, complete with his face plastered on billboards and commercial features. Imagine the inner spiritual work he had to do in order to overcome the criticism, the shame, the guilt, and the ridicule he received. He made a choice to be a voice for change, long before he could be sure that he or his career would live on. Magic Johnson's career trajectory might be linear, but his life is not.

Professional success is not your greatest purpose. It can be a powerful and important part of your vision but try looking at this another way. Vision is not simply revealed by what you do. It is revealed in what you learn, what you overcome, what you value, and what you realize along the way. It is not always picture perfect.

7-Perfectly Written. "Write the Vision and Make It Plain" is often quoted with the takeaway "all I have to do is write it down, and it will happen." Let's take a closer look at this saying which comes from the Bible in the book of Habakkuk Chapter 2. This is not a biblical study of the text but a few important contextual observations on a well-known scripture that has turned into a popular spiritual phrase about vision. A closer look at the text reveals important lessons on vision that are not as regularly espoused along with the positive cliché. I encourage you to study this independently and talk with others of faith in your spiritual community, such as your pastor, small group members, and friends.

When God speaks these words to the prophet Habakkuk, it is not to inspire him for weight loss, a professional promotion, or relationship goals. Honestly, I spent years hearing, repeating, and singing this phrase before ever reading it in context. When I did, it was quite eye opening. For women of faith like myself, I believe it is important to grow spiritually so that your vision can be in alignment with truth. This verse is not about a perfectly clear vision but rather about the long hardships of community progress. Here are three observations that I found significant when considering this scripture as inspiration for your envisioning experience.

Adversity. Having a vision won't mean you avoid adversity, but it will help you navigate it. If God's conversation with Habakkuk is the first vision board, let's just say it wasn't your typical party. It was more like a desperate prayer for direction, guidance, and a glimmer of hope. Habakkuk is the prophet who God told to write the vision and it was vividly clear. But the vision he saw was not a happy one. It included great suffering before the coveted blessings that he and his people wanted from God. They were to go through this period of turmoil to get rid of attitudes, material possessions, and beliefs that were harmful and would not allow them to move into the realm of greatness that they were capable of becoming. Having a clear and powerful vision does not mean you will escape adversity. In fact, sometimes encountering adversity brings attention to the things you need to purge from your life in order to move forward. Get it up and out of the way. Detox the junk that doesn't belong and know that prioritizing your vision may bring with it more character building challenges. Therefore, be aware that when those challenges arise, it is not a shock or a complete surprise. It is not always a roadblock to keep you from the vision but could be just a hurdle you have to cross in order to get closer to your vision.

Time. Your vision will come to you or be expanded at the appointed time. This scripture refers to a divine encounter. It is not a vision of this person's imagination. It is a vision revealed from God. That means, as the rapper Drake says, it is God's plan. In the passage, it talks about the appointed time. God says numerous times that it may seem to take a while for things to happen, but just wait because everything will happen at the right time. Keep that in mind as you walk in your vision because there are times when things will come to pass quickly and effortlessly. That can be attractive in this fast-paced culture of microwaves, instant coffee, and one-day shipping. Society says, "I want it now!" No, for real. The Grubhub commercial jingle goes, "I want it all, and I want it now." It can also be deceptive to declare fast results as the model of success when it comes to vision. What appears to be an overnight success is typically the culmination of a longer, less visible journey. Be invested in your vision for the long haul. It doesn't mean that everything has to take forever, but the timing is not under your control. Some things will happen fast. Others will happen slowly. But it will all happen at the appointed time.

Personal vs. Collective Vision. Your vision is not all about you. Emphasis on the word all. The vision in the book of Habakkuk is given to one person and meant to apply to many people. In fact, it applied to an entire nation of people. It was a message to Habakkuk AND for his community. When vision is discussed, it is often spoken of as a singular experience about one person. I like to imagine vision as a more holistic experience where it represents what you hope and believe, as well as those who you will impact and influence. It is also about those who will impact and influence you. Your vision is about you, but it is not all about you. Real talk, you do not live alone on a deserted island. What happens to you impacts your family and the community around you. What you do affects those in your sphere of influence. The same is true in reverse. Those with whom you fellowship with and what they do has an impact on you. A significant part of daily life is interacting with the people, so it is important to observe and pay attention. You are in a community, a family, a church, a neighborhood, a country that needs you in it. Look outside of yourself to see how you can connect who you are with where you are.

We crave community. For heart-centered women like you, who care deeply about others, casting a vision will lead you to consider and pray about how your unique place in the world has a direct impact on those around you. "How can I serve? How can I love well?" These are questions that can help you deepen your vision to reflect your leadership and purpose.

Better than perfect, real vision is about knowing that every day you are showing up continuously and consistently connected to a bigger picture of your giant life. That the ebbs and flows, the imperfections and the challenges are all working together for your good because God is talking about you when the scripture says that *all things are working for the good of those who love God and are called according to His purpose* – which is to love and serve. Real vision is about knowing that every day you are showing up, gaining clarity, and using wisdom to be who God created you to be.

Reality Check Your Vision: What are the myths you learned about vision? Which myth described above will you release immediately? How does the pursuit of perfectionism show up in your real life and hinder your progress?

Chapter 8

PERMISSION TO VISION

"You're not going to have everything you need from the start. Your provisions are waiting for you as you take the steps towards your impossible dream."

-Peter J. Bone, Achieve the Impossible[vii]

Now that you have unpacked the pesky little p-word, "perfect," as it pertains to vision, let's discover a new p-word; a much more important one: permission. If you have walked a mile in similar shoes and have been in search of vision, there are many ways for you to connect with it. Journaling, shifting my mindset, and creating a personalized vision board worked for me.

While I was rebuilding my life and relationships, I started leading professional development trainings for corporate and non-profit teams. It occurred to me that many of the practices I was using for professional development with organizational leaders, employees, and non- profit executives, could also be used for their personal development. After all, majority of workplace conflict is 1) toxic exchanges with a manager or co-worker i.e. relationships and 2) employees feeling stuck in their jobs which was connected to vision, mission, and goals.

Whether personally or professionally, at work or at home, these were issues that every human being had to face. But the goal of a business bringing me in to conduct a training was to have the team successfully tackle these issues so that the organization could flourish along with the employees. In other words, the goal was to turn these employees into leaders! When I realized that, I knew I needed to try a comprehensive approach in my trainings to talk to teams about personal AND professional success.

I experimented with blending the two, using vision boards in professional trainings and using strategic analysis tools when I worked one-on-one with clients. This worked well. Not only was I receiving feedback from my client, the employers, I was receiving tons of valuable feedback from the employees themselves, noting that they never thought their jobs even cared about who they were outside of work. They hadn't felt free to have a vision for themselves outside of work, let alone to share it and receive support from colleagues. This was especially true for women I worked with in these sessions. Though they had good reputations as hard workers, they played it small. They'd chosen to suppress rather than express any of the big life visions they merely dreamed about but had not yet the courage to say openly. The opportunity for them to connect their personal vision to their professional career provided the freedom to get excited about their whole lives and go confidently in the direction of their vision.

After years of consulting, coaching, and leading workshops, I discovered three areas that limit women in their vision: constant comparison, perfectionism, and limiting beliefs – it's the kind of baggage that weights more than luggage at the airport. This disconnection from vision can be summed up in one word: permission. While affirmation is always appreciated from those you respect such as your spouse/partner, your mentor, or your employer, permission is only needed from yourself.

Dear heart, if you need it, this is your permission. Give yourself permission to vision. Personalized and Authentic. Accomplishing goals when you don't know who you are is an exercise in futility that leaves you feeling empty inside. You end up constantly striving to finish your long to-do list, invested in accomplishing a task, but for all your hard work, you remain unfulfilled, exhausted, and unclear what it's all for. Being busy and being fulfilled are two different things.

Give yourself the permission to let go of all the baggage you carry to protect yourself from being criticized as a "know it all," or a smart aleck, or anything else said to you in an effort to make you play just a little bit smaller. You don't need that type of negative energy in your life, which perpetuates fear over freedom. But you, with your wild soft heart, full of empathy for others, sharing an encouraging word to many but have few words left for yourself, with your giant dreams, it is time to walk on the other side. Allow yourself to fully express the desires of your heart. Your vision board can be a fantastic symbol of the vision you have for your giant life. But as long as you hide it, the symbolism is lost.

Reality Check: What area(s) of your life do you need to give yourself permission to be free? Circle all that apply. What does it mean to give yourself permission in these areas of your life?

- Permission to create an authentic vision that is a true reflection of yourself, not just a collection of pretty pictures.
- Permission to connect your personal and professional life so that you can honor your whole self
- Permission to slow down the pace of your life and take a much-needed break
- Permission to take a journey of self-discovery so that your vision is rooted in your values and personal leadership, not just in the current roles and responsibilities you have.
- Permission to dedicate time to your vision and engage with it regularly
- Something else_____

Chapter 9

THE VEHICLE FOR YOUR VISION

Vision is not simply revealed by what you do. It is revealed in what you learn, what you overcome, what you value, and what you realize along the way.
#FreeYourRealVision
-Alexandria @YesSheLeads

Your vision needs a you. You are the vehicle for your vision. You carry it with you with courage and commitment. You are the element that makes your vision unique. It's not your job or your degree. No one can do exactly what you do or how you will do it. However, your career is one way for you to implement your vision. In the United States, we spend just as much time, if not more, working on a job or a business as we do at home with family. It is a significant aspect of daily life. So, it makes sense that your vision will show up in your work. Yet, unlike the path of previous generations, most Gen X, Millennials, and Gen Z's will not get hired at 25 and retire at 65, spending a lifetime at one single company. Sometimes, a pivot in your career will call for reinvention in what you do. In Chapter 7, I shared with you that vision embraces reinvention. Since vision is not a perfect path, it does not run from the pivot but finds ways to align values with a new opportunity. Remember, your vision is a compass, not a roadmap. It helps you to know which direction you are going and helps you stay on course, but it does not give you coordinates to your exact destination. A real vision is one where you discover as you transform.

Some may prefer the edited and polished look of a successful life versus the reality. It is like the difference of choosing between two bowls of fruit. As each bowl is laid out in front of you, you notice they both have an apple, a banana, and some grapes. They both look good. So, which do you choose? What if I told you that one bowl is artificial wax fruit and the other was real authentic fruit from a tree? Would that help you to decide? See, the main purpose of fruit is not to look good, so while the look might be appealing, it isn't the deciding factor. The deciding factor is taste. In that category, authentic beats artificial every single time.

Real vision is more concerned with what life really is versus what it may appear to be to others looking in from the outside. The only question you need to continuously ask yourself is, "Is this aligned with my values not just my title or position?" "Am I doing the best that I can with the information that I have?" Here are four examples of people whose stories exemplify the career pivot that led to reinvention. These examples are wonderful and imperfect people who taught me vision is more about the person than the position or the popularity. The position can change. Can you still be committed to your vision when it is not the popular decision? The popularity can wane because people don't agree with your decision to pivot. Remember, your career, roll, or position do not solely define you. You are the vehicle for your real vision. Take your values and your vision everywhere you go.

Allow me to introduce you to Doctor Shaquille Rashaun O'Neil aka NBA All-Star Shaq. And yes, he actually does have a Doctor of Education in Human Resource Development from Barry University in Miami, Florida. And that's exactly the point. Dr. O'Neil has…ok let me stop playing games. Shaq has embraced reinvention as a part of life. His fans might say he is a great, influential, and powerful basketball player. He might say he wants to be a great, influential, and powerful person. In addition to his career as an athlete and a number of advanced degrees, Shaq is rather diverse. He has been a rapper, an actor, a reserve law enforcement officer, and an EDM (electronic dance music) DJ – think along the lines of techno and house music. That doesn't even include his business ventures with restaurants and real estate, or the various brand endorsements that aren't related to his long career as an athlete. Although he is best known for his career on the court, he did not lock himself into that single role. He has reinvented himself through his career time and time again. In each choice, you can see his values shine through. He takes that intensity, laughter, adventure, and high impact performance into everything.

Marguerite Annie Johnson is an American artist who has done everything from plays to documentaries to opera and more. For many years, she was a popular Calypso dancer in San Francisco in the 1950's. She was also a dance partner with a young Alvin Ailey as he launched his famous career. For all of her dear friendships with important influences like that of Malcolm X, James Baldwin, and Martin Luther King, Marguerite grew up in a difficult and abusive environment. Having endured sexual abuse, she actually didn't speak for several years during her childhood because she feared her voice. Marguerite had an enduring passion for social justice and civil rights. For this reason, many of her projects focused on racial identity, racism, and Black women. She coordinated many fundraisers for the Southern Christian Leadership Convention, inspiring other artists to get involved by performing and helping to fund community movements. She traveled around the world and lived in Sweden, Egypt, and Ghana at different times in her life. She had such a colorful career, writing music for the likes of Roberta Flack and receiving a Grammy for recording her poetry. Marguerite also wrote a number of books that are actually quite famous. Perhaps you'd recognize a book *I Know Why The Caged Bird Sings* if you looked it up under her stage name: Maya Angelou. Every semester that I taught the Leadership Class at Spelman College, I amazed and confused my students who only had a picture of the poet laureate as the regal and elder Ms. Angelou; many weren't prepared to see her as a barefoot dancer with a halter-top on. Yet, each stage she stepped on, whether as a dancer, or singer, or poet, she brought with her the arts. Although best known for her poetry and novels, Maya Angelou lived her life as a consummate artist, and the world was her stage.

Author Marshawn Evans shares in her book *Believe Bigger*, that her story was anything but linear. In fact, she went from being a beauty pageant queen, to law school, to a finalist on The Apprentice, to a practicing attorney, to starting a sports management company, and finally to a best-selling author coaching women in business and life. Marshawn admits she did not see how any of these things were connected at the time, but she knew that God could see what she could not see; she believed that somehow, it would all work out if she just continued to trust God and lean on her faith. Well, it did. She can now see that in every situation, she was able to use her gifts to amplify the message of others and advocate for those felt like they didn't have a voice. Marshawn also built an invaluable network, personal and professional, along the way.

Les Brown, one of the world's most renowned motivational speakers, mastered reinvention because his story is nothing close to picture perfect. He and his twin brother were given up by their biological parents. They were later adopted and loved by a strong spirited mother with a ton of heart but not a ton of money. He worked for years to overcome the obstacles to achieve his dream of becoming a self-taught DJ & radio personality. Once he was in his career, he realized that he wanted to do something that had greater impact. Then Les Brown spent a decade making the transition into the world of public speaking which is what he is best known for all around the world. His story is not linear. But he valued connecting with people and learned great orator skills along the way which he was able to use for his vision and life.

When I realized that my path was not expected to be picture perfect and that my non-linear journey could still lead me to my vision, it was a huge epiphany. Despite my challenges and setbacks, I began to see how God has continuously moved in my life. Upon further reflection, it confirmed for me that I was right where I needed to be. I am created to live a real vision for my life, and so are you!

Vision Tracing. Has this ever happened to you? You see something you really like. It's different. It's bold. It's totally you. A new hairstyle, a new pair of shoes, or even a new car color. You buy it and you are so excited about it! But then, you start seeing your beloved item pop up everywhere! It's like after you actually see what it is that you want, you start seeing it everywhere!

After a successful career as an educator and entrepreneur, I felt compelled to refocus on my writing as the center of my career. This came as a shock, but only to me, as many of my dear friends and family felt like it was a natural progression. I, on the other hand, did not. This is why it is incredibly important to have a supportive community around to lovingly pour into you. They can help you bring out what you don't already see. They can hold up the mirror so you can see yourself clearly. If I had continued to be surrounded by the same circle of people from when I was younger, it would have taken me even longer to get to a place where I felt brave and supported enough to pursue this aspect of my vision. As my health coach and friend Karlyn says, "Love is a verb. I am the subject." I learned that God loves me. I learned to love me. And I learned to only accept people in my inner circle who showed loving actions towards me. Bullying, verbal abuse, and neglect had to go. Not only was it unhealthy but being surrounded by that stifled my creativity.

Support is love in action. So, when I announced this shift, my inner circle simply said, "Sounds great. What book are you writing first?" Internally, I was shooketh! Oh, I had plenty of book ideas to write about. But after building two businesses, getting married, and becoming a mother, I trembled a bit at the thought of a pivot. I must have failed somewhere along the way, right? I should have seen this coming! I should have been better prepared. And now, here I am, starting over. Again! *Where was this revelation a few years ago?* I sulked, sort of talking to myself as I whimpered on the pillow. Low key, I was rolling my eyes at God. As if to answer, the Lord began to show me all the years of writing that I had done, and all of it was leading up to this. I created what I call "Vision Tracing" that focuses on one aspect of life and plots age points to see when you remember gaining interest in the subject resulting in a timeline. Instead of looking ahead to future projections, it was an opportunity to look back on what was already done and truly see how far you have come. You can do vision tracing for multiple subjects as your vision may contain more than one component. Here is my vision trace for creative writing, the area where my vision is currently being expanded:

Activity: Vision Tracing

Subject: Creative Writing

Age 0-10

- 1st place winner at oratorical speech competitions
- Started reading novels for fun
- Started writing short stories

Age 11-20

- Started writing poems
- Started a poetry group and began writing and performing poetry
- Published my first commissioned poem
- Co-wrote a play and lyrics for songs/rap music

Age 21-30

- Wrote and published a book of poetry and short stories
- Wrote 100 pages of a novel one summer and never finished it
- Started writing for online magazines and blogs

- Served as editor for numerous projects for artists and organizations
- Published a book length research thesis on artists as culture advocates
- Burned out from academic writing and avoided writing ANYTHING creative
- Launched a personal blog a few years later

Age 30-Now

- Wanted to write a book but didn't write a book
- Really wanted to write a book
- Really, really wanted to write a book and built up confidence to pick a topic
- Started writing a book and considered the first draft a mild hot mess in a dumpster fire and quit.
- Un-quit because I realized this is exactly what I want to do to carry the message of creative empowerment to millennial women of faith in this season of my life, and God is pointing his finger in this direction.
- And then finally, wrote this book

I was surprised to find out how equipped I was to shift my focus toward writing. Over the course of my life, I had many snapshots of creative writing that individually didn't amount to an entire career. However, when brought together and placed side by side, they created a large collage where then I was able to see my career differently. This activity empowered me to go from agitated to activated. I got so excited because I realized that this change was not coming out of the blue. It was in my blind spot which is why I didn't see it. I had been in an incubation process for a long time subconsciously getting ready for this. Because writing was in a blind spot for so long, it was not really part of the vision I had for myself. I remember as a young girl being constantly reminded that writers, and creatives in general, don't make money. They just make art and then have to find other types of work to make a living. As a result, writing full time wasn't what I saw myself doing. Writing could be part of my job, an assignment for a client, a freelance article, the path to a degree, or a hobby. But writing couldn't be a career. I saw it as a strategic tool, not as a creative gift.

Besides, writers spend their lives in isolation typing in a basement staring at a computer screen all their lives, I thought. *I'm a woman of the people, not the computer screen*, I protested. I crave connection with loving, down to earth, encouraging folks who know how to keep the faith and keep it real about life's ups and downs. Yet, after a few years of being a stay-at-home mom talking to a toddler all day, I'd learned to be without the company of adult conversation all the time. Any mother who has been home with a toddler for more than seventy-two hours straight will tell you they happily delight in the beauty of complete silence as they stare at a phone ringing on vibrate certain that whatever the call is about can surely be made into a text message.

Then I transitioned from stay-at-home mom to work-from-home wife assisting my husband, building a business from the ground up. I'd changed. Sitting at home typing for hours on end alone, with no one to chat with all day wasn't as foreign to me as it once was. Suddenly, I could see myself at my desk, typing away, publishing books online, signing copies of my latest project at an author talk. The learning and changing that happened over time in my life prepared me to expand the vision I had for myself into one where I welcomed this transformation. It was further confirmation that this plot twist was right on time.

Vision boards are only one way to capture your vision. Since being a full-time author was not in my line of sight, it wasn't on my vision board. However, upon reflection, there are other things that alluded to this desire indirectly including book authors and book covers that I found inspirational. Keep in mind that vision is a collection of many goals, and a fulfillment of a life lived, full of values in action. Sharing big ideas, communication, and creative learning are all important life values for me. It was only through the vision tracing activity above that I was able to shift my perspective to see becoming an author as a way for me to live my values. In fact, these are the activities I encourage you to do.

Reality Check Your Vision. What could you discover about yourself if you did your own vision timeline activity? What is hiding in your blind spot? Now it's time for you to trace your vision. Select a topic in your life that you are getting curious about or want to develop. Document any areas of your life where this subject has shown up in the past and create your own vision trace.

Chapter 10

VISION STARTS RIGHT HERE

"I am learning every day to allow the space between where I am and where I want to be to inspire me and not terrify me." – Tracee Ellis Ross

S**tart showing up instead of busy and stuck**. Many amazing and creative women refuse to participate in the visioning process. It is important to show up for yourself, but that can be a huge challenge if you feel stuck. On more than one occasion, I have listened to women express apprehension about imagining a powerful vision for their lives. From vision board parties to the intimate one-on-one conversations, I've sat in corners of rooms large and small listening to the whispers of women leaders who are almost afraid to envision something new. The weight of so many responsibilities, hectic busy schedules, and the silent commitment they've made to ignore the desires of their heart has them feeling stuck. And just like that, your beautiful ideas go from start to stuck as indecision and paralysis of analysis set in.

A busy life does not equal a meaningful life. For many women leaders, seeking work/life balance seems impossible and the situation is dire. It's like the character in your favorite scary movie walking to the front door of the abandoned haunted house and you commence to fuss at the screen, "Do NOT go there!!" Well, here we are, and I am saying to you "Do NOT go there!!" If you are overwhelmed by the great list of things you are doing and decide to prioritize them but can't, because, "everybody needs me right now," there is a glitch in *The Matrix* and it's time to *Get Out*. If you feel stuck or beholden to the roles you play, yet remain utterly drained and completely unfulfilled, there is an iceberg ahead and you are the *Titanic*. Shift course now!

It can be dangerous out here in these busy body streets. It is deceptive because being busy is praised in our society, especially with women. Women are applauded for being hard working, dependable, and, here it comes…strong. That sounds like a Cadillac commercial from the 1980's more than a person. Newsflash! We are not machines. You want to look like a goal-getter instead of a "gold-digger" and I get that.

But when being busy leads to exhaustion, burn out, fatigue, and you still end up feeling stuck, it's a problem.

Being busy and being productive are not the same thing. While attending the annual business seminar with Lamar Tyler of *Traffic, Sales, and Profit*, I had a powerful reality check that felt more like a karate kick to the throat. Lamar talked about all the reasons why creative entrepreneurs succeed or give up on their business using his favorite sentence "Done is better than perfect." He goes on to talk about how overthinking was the main culprit for many entrepreneurs on their pathway to success as he shared the following quote which initiated an important mindset shift for me:

> **"You're not stuck**. You're just committed to certain patterns of behavior because they helped you in the past. Now those behaviors have become more harmful than helpful. The reason why **you can't** move forward is because you keep applying an old formula to a new level in your life. Change the formula to get a different result." -Emily Maroutian[viii]

Mind blown. "Is it possible that I'm not stuck?" I asked myself. It was all too familiar to my own journey. Like many of the business women and men in the room, I recognized that I needed to cultivate a real vision for my life, take better care of God's child, nourish my soul, and honor my creative voice.

But when did I have time to do all of that? You see, I broke up with years of emotionally and verbally abusive relationships in my past. I spent even more time breaking up with my own self-limiting beliefs and self-sabotage; yet, when I closed my eyes, the woman I went to sleep with was a far cry from where I wanted to be.

But God, how am I ever going to get there?

What I was really saying deep in my heart was, *Oh God, I'm never going to get there!* It felt overwhelming.

Fear spoke clearly back to me: *You need to just give up and avoid this entirely. Things will be easier for you. Learn to accept that in life, it is what it is. Don't make things hard for yourself.* It is seductively appealing. A Netflix and Chill kind of life, lounging around watching episode after episode of other people live their lives and using their gifts for its creative purpose while you wait for nothing great to happen to you. Fear was loud; my determination was louder. *Nah, I'm good.* After a while, I felt even more sure of this truth. *I am not stuck*, I announced to myself. I began to entertain a new question: *What if another way forward is possible and how do I get there?*

Start Fresh. A fresh start can interrupt old patterns and give you a new perspective for vision in your life. My task was simple. If I feel stuck, I need to interrupt the pattern and make a different choice. One of the areas I felt most stuck in was an unhealthy lifestyle. I started interrupting my patterns with small baby steps like cooking at home and packing my lunch so that I could have access to healthy food instead of being stuck with a vending machine to fuel my body for twelve-hour work days. This gave me more energy and focus. Two messages guided me and became my mantra. Arthur Ashe says, "Start where you are; use what you have; do what you can." And the bible verse "I can do all things through Christ who strengthens me." (Philippians 4:13). These small changes opened up the door to change other areas of my life.

Start Discovering Your Thing. I have had a bone disorder since childhood that causes severe pain, primarily in my legs. It caused me to miss school and stop playing sports as a pre-teen; so, working out has always been tough for me. But the lack of exercise caused my muscles to feel weak. I tried running groups for women, knowing my pace meant I would be in the last group to complete the run. The women in the group were very encouraging towards me; however, these women were running marathons on their day off. I'm serious, an actual 10K just for fun! I realized this wasn't "my thing." I was proud of their fitness success, but I had to discover my own path in order to make it sustainable. I needed to find something that worked for *me* so that I didn't give up. That's when I discovered groups like Girl Trek, who focus on walking as healing drawing inspiration from Harriet Tubman on her walk towards freedom. It truly changed my life and allowed me to reclaim my health by walking every day. Over time, I was able to build the confidence and courage to do bigger things like decide to leave my nine-to-five job, pursuing full-time entrepreneurship; and open my heart to love again after years of romantic uncertainty.

Start being true to your word. Start being true to your word by searching for your enthusiastic yes. If it is not a strong and powerful yes, then it's really a no. In a season where you need to create space for your vision to grow, you must yield less to the demands of others. "Maybe," and "Ok I guess," is not "Yes!" Those answers are not enthusiastic agreements, and too many inauthentic answers crowd your schedule and your personal space. A clear yes (and a clear no) will make following up or following through much easier. If you are not used to setting this boundary with yourself and others, you may find that you default to answering yes, even when you don't really mean it.

Don't let anyone force you into an answer. If they are asking you to do something, that means you have to give them permission to proceed. Here are two things that I do when I am confronted with a request and am not prepared to immediately say yes:

#1 – My automatic response is, "Let me get back to you in 24 hours."

#2 – Sit down with my calendar and determine if I can fully commit with an enthusiastic yes.

Being put on the spot to answer right away creates the pressure to just say yes, whether you mean it or not. Don't do it, because nine times out of ten it is not a life or death situation. Don't let their urgency become your emergency. If they respond and say they can't wait 24 hours to hear back from you and they need to know right away, then tell them confidently that without time to efficiently check your schedule, the answer is no. Why? Because the reality is that it is only partially about the appointments on your schedule. It is also about how much you have to give to a situation that is not your top priority.

Your resources are your time, your money, and your energy, too. So, take the 24 hours to think about your response before you instinctively say yes. That gives you plenty of time to consider all of your priorities. An enthusiastic yes is powerful because it sounds like the staff at Chick-Fil-A: "It's my pleasure" versus "I can't wait for this to be over." Wouldn't it be nice to accept an opportunity to show up and help others in a way that allows you to give freely with joy in your heart and in your service? It changes the dynamic of showing up out of obligation versus being present because you can and want to help. This will limit you from cancelling plans at the last minute or ghosting your friends to avoid a commitment. This is invigorating and fills you up. Protect your energy so that you can be a woman of your word and leave space for you to grow in your vision, instead of constantly feeling obligated to respond with a yes to everyone except yourself.

Start speaking positively about yourself to yourself. Eliminate negative self-talk by recognizing it in your thoughts before they become words. If you do one hundred things right and one thing wrong, your focus should not be fixed on the error. Perfectionism is a trap to pull you into feeling inadequate and stop you from moving forward. This can show up as procrastination, or scrutinizing your work, even after you have finished it, constantly being hard on yourself in the name of "needing to get it right."

When it happens, interrupt yourself. Change your language and re-frame the words.

"I screwed up. I suck! I'm such a mess. God, I always do this!"

Stop yourself mid-sentence or as soon as you recognize it. Tell your-self the truth. Reframe.

"No, that's not true. I am not a mess, and I don't ALWAYS make mis-takes like this. Everyone makes mistakes and I am human. I am getting better and growing stronger because I am learning something new."

Now speak positively about yourself.

"I am better because of this experience. I am glad that I tried and will continue to improve."

Start embracing a growth mindset. There are books dedicated to growth versus fixed mindset. One of the most respected is called *Mind-set: The New Psychology of Success* by Carol S. Dweck. With a fixed mindset, a person reaches limits quickly of what they can do in the face of adversity. In other words, it is easy to get stuck because the one or two options that they tried didn't work out, so then they stop. The growth mindset is seeing that same situation and considering all the possibilities. Then they explore all of those options until they find something that works. A growth mindset is useful when facing per-sonal and professional challenges, creatively using tools that have worked well for you in the past, as well as discovering new tools to solve problems. A growth mindset helps you to approach a challenge as an opportunity to grow rather than an obstacle meant to stop you.

Start Accepting Compliments. Do you find it difficult to accept a compliment?

Them: "Wow, you look nice today!"

You: "What are you talking about? Look at this new growth. I need to make a hair appointment asap. And you see the polish is starting to chip on my nails."

Them: "Cute outfit!"

You: "Girl, this is so old. And I got the shoes on sale."

Ma'am, please stop putting yourself down when others are lifting you up. This is along the lines of eliminating negative self-talk. It is absolutely okay to receive appropriate praise. While you are at it, share the love and give a compliment or two as well.

Start Embracing a Lifetime Instead of a Strict Timeline. Remember that you are on time for your life. You want vision to draw you closer to a lifetime of purpose fulfilled, not haunt you with nagging thought *"I should've done it already!"* These thoughts need to be conquered in the firm truth, so here it is. You are on time for your life! Everything you have learned along the way will aid you in cultivating your future. In fact, longing to perfectly edit one's past has a way of getting you stuck there in the past. Value your journey of a lifetime. It is a rich tapestry of your history, your joys, your sorrows, your journey. Instead of wishing you could change the past, embrace the lessons that you have learned. Take a look at how you can apply that information in this season of your life. Acknowledge that because you learned so much in the past, your learning curve gives you an advantage. Now, you are able to move through a process twice as fast! Don't be so quick to call the past a mistake. Perhaps you are just done with that assignment. Give yourself some grace. Give yourself permission to say, "I got what I needed" and "Thank you, now I'm ready to move on."

Start Embracing Change. It is important to know that when things change, it's not always easy, but it is absolutely worth it. "It's not the situation, but how you respond," as my uncle Joe, a pastor, has said to me often during marriage counseling sessions.

Ever feel like you are failing in an area of your life? Sometimes, it's not even your fault because you were forced into a transition. No one ever puts, "get fired from a job" or "home foreclosure" on their vision board. It's the kind of thing that makes you want to give up and throw in the towel. That's how I felt when I was let go from my dream job. Yet, difficult life transitions allow you to choose how you will see this opportunity. Will you perform, conform, or transform?

After working for a year and a half at my dream job on a social justice program for college leaders at a women's college, the program lost its funding. My initial response was not to embrace change at all. I was hurt and angry about it. It wasn't just in the moment but for months afterward. My hurt was especially amplified after I learned that I was pregnant. I was big mad. And, I got stuck there, in pain from a challenging pregnancy and in my feelings because life was not at all working out like I'd planned or imagined. Every day I had to apply for another job or go to an interview, I lamented on how hard this was and fuss about why this was all happening to me. Who wants to try to be impressive, nauseous, and pregnant on an interview with your potential new boss? It was difficult to say the least.

After being bitter for a while, I realized something needed to change because this situation was my new reality. I chose to shift my perspective in order to move forward. I was very sick for six months of my pregnancy, going to doctors' appointments two to three days out of the week. I started to see the benefit of not having a high stress job during this season of my life. For the first time since I'd left the position, I felt gratitude for my situation. I thanked God for my job and all that it had provided me as I began to embrace the new reality. I witnessed first-hand how deciding to see my situation changed everything. You get to decide as well. You get to decide to get up and lead your life even when you don't feel like it. "Feeling like it" is not a prerequisite for action. Change will happen with or without your permission. It is what you do with it that matters the most. As my father Gregory said a million times when I was growing up, "Change is mandatory, but growth is optional. If you want to be great, you must grow." My father also named me after the great conqueror and king Alexander the Great as to motivate me to fully take over the world, so as a child, I took his advice seriously. It is a sobering truth. Embrace change so that you can grow into your greatness.

Start Making Meaning of the Shift. You can go through it all; your whole world can be turned upside down. However, you get to decide if you will make some meaning of this shift. You get to decide if you will choose to learn something from this situation. You get to decide if you will ask God to grant you the wisdom and the knowledge to move forward and butterfly this thing. Yes, I did just make butterfly a verb. Once you embrace change, it is much easier to turn obstacles into opportunities.

After I embraced the change of pregnancy and the loss of this dream job, I was then able to make some meaning of this shift. I could see the benefits clearly. It gave me the opportunity to rest for my health and the health of my child. It gave me the opportunity to return to the classroom as an Adjunct Professor teaching Leadership and Public Speaking classes part-time versus a highly rigorous full-time administrative position. Once my daughter was born, being laid off also gave me the opportunity to go on "maternity leave" for as long as I deemed necessary, which I could not really have done in my previous position. It was the postpartum rest I didn't know I needed. I was able to make meaning out of that shift so that I could receive the most from the experience.

Start at Any Age. Don't be afraid to pivot in your life, business, or career. I have had my fair share of personal and professional pivots that have created opportunities for me to learn new skills, build new relationships, and broaden my horizons. In some ways, it expanded my vision. In other ways, it strengthened the resolve for my vision. In Chapter 9, I shared a few examples of the pivot. I want to specifically make that connection to age. In girlhood, women are quite often told their age makes them naïve and inexperienced. On the other age extreme, women of a certain age more seasoned with life experience are often considered less relevant and their wisdom "dated" by societies standards. It seems there is never a right time for a woman to start something new. Good thing women with real vision don't need to agree with society's standards to make their next move. I want to share two stories of incredible women who hit their stride in an unexpected time in life.

Dorothy Steele, a retired IRS (Internal Revenue Service) employee and grandmother, decided to become an actor at the age of 88 years old while living in Atlanta. While in her 70's, she attended a senior citizens center that produced plays for the residents. Dorothy took a few roles every now and then for fun. Ten years later, her hobby turned into a full-time career with a few reoccurring roles on television. However, it was at the beautiful age of 91 that she received an audition which threw her career into overdrive when she landed an important part on the film *Black Panther* as a member of the King's Council. In a 2018 Washington Post interview, Dorothy offered her sage words of advice, "Hopefully, somebody who at 55 or 60 has decided, 'This is all I can do,' they will realize they have 35 more years to get things together," Steel said. "Start now. It's never too late. ... Keep your mind open and keep faith in yourself that you can do this thing. All you have to do is step out there."[ix]

There's another woman whose story I'm quite fond of. She is a British woman who was working for the nonprofit Amnesty International. After becoming a mother and getting a divorce, she pivoted into a completely different direction. She ended up writing fantasy books about magic and wizards, a rather unusual subject. Turns out, her work found hundreds of millions of fans (500 million actually) who believed in magic too. Eventually, her little book project became a global phenomenon and found its way to *The New York Times* Bestseller list. Her work went on to be adapted as both book and film series, breaking record numbers for film and is considered the best-selling book series worldwide. Her name is J.K. Rowling, the author of Harry Potter.

Start allowing yourself to vision. You are a vision in progress. Therefore, there must at least be two things: vision and progress. Start allowing yourself to have a vision, no matter what your circumstances are. Start small and choose one area of your life that you can begin "seeing" differently. Then, over time, strengthen that and add new areas. Choose to be courageous and start doing some of the activities that are provided in this book to help you strengthen access to your vision in each area of your life.

Reality Check Your Vision: Are you a person that has a tough time making progress on your creative ideas? What do you do to get motivated again and take action when you find yourself stuck? Which Vision In Progress principle resonated with you the most?

Chapter 11

VISION TRANSFORMATION:
RISE LIKE THE TREE

"Without a compelling vision, you will discover there is
no reason to go through the pain of change."
-Brian Moran, The 12 Week Year[x]

A s a visionary, there are three seasons of transformation that speak to the different stages of a vision in real time. This adds to your authenticity. Every single person in the world goes through challenges or unpredictable circumstances. However, what you learn from them, or learn while you are still in them, sets you apart and allows the experiences to empower and encourage instead of discourage you. You may find yourself in one of these three transformational seasons right now.

1. Rise – a season of growth and consistency.
2. Lead – a season of change and metamorphosis.
3. Shine – a season of celebration, sharing, and flourishing.

In fact, you may realize you are experiencing more than one season at the same time. You can be rising in your romantic relationships and shining in your career. That's okay. Wherever you are, my hope is for you to feel more confident and less confused when you recognize yourself in one of these three seasons. In fact, anticipate that these seasons will occur as part of the change in your life; and armed with this information, be prepared to stay the course, committed to living out your vision. This is an ongoing process of refining your goals and plans as life happens. Do not be bound by arbitrary deadlines. This is your life's work, and you are in a process that has success, joy, contentment, and challenges. Be resilient in your faith of who God created you to be, in and out of season. Remember that you are a vision in progress.

The Life of Trees. I love trees. In fact, because of my above average height, I have been compared to trees for much of my life. I decided to turn this quasi insult on its head and embrace it. Yes, I am like a tree. Tall. Strong, with roots that run deep. In fact, I became fascinated with them in elementary school. The California Redwood stood out to me the most. It is the tallest tree in North America. They can grow to be more than three hundred feet, only slightly taller than me!

I recently learned of another beautiful tree that amazes me: the Chinese Bamboo. It grows differently than most other trees. It is unique because it spends five years underground, existing only as seed and roots. It doesn't begin to show signs of growth until it has been planted and watered for five years consistently. Every day. Can you imagine doing one thing every single day for five years straight without seeing any growth? Then, after five long years, over a matter of just a few weeks, it rapidly grows to eighty (80) feet tall. When I first learned of this, I wondered, *How can something stay so incredibly small with no signs of growth for so long?* And then I wondered *How can it grow so quickly in a matter of weeks to the height of a building?* Well, that's the way God created it. That's the way it was designed. It takes great patience to endure such a lengthy process.

Be Consistent. Just like people, trees have their own unique cycles of life. Sometimes, they grow little by little over time, and you can see the progress clearly like the California Redwood. But that is not always the case. Sometimes, life is like a Chinese Bamboo. If you stopped watering it after year one, two, or three because you didn't see any results, you would stop short of what is required to make this tree grow. All would be lost, and the tree would never rise above the ground. Consistency is patience plus action. With consistency, you will see results. Isn't that what's happening in life? When immediate results are not visible, it's easy to give up and deprive yourself of the key resources that you need to grow! This is exactly what the Rise season is about. No matter what you have been going through or how long you have been in this season, I want you to hear me clearly. Do not stop watering your vision. Do not stop nourishing yourself. Do not give up. Rest and reset, but don't give up on what God has placed in your heart. One last interesting fact about the Chinese Bamboo tree. It is one of the strongest trees in the world. Bamboo is stronger than steel. It doesn't easily break. Perhaps after all those years of being consistently nourished, it can withstand anything and keep growing. Be consistent so you can grow strong too.

Be a visionary. When you look at seeds, you need to see trees. The seeds of your vision will grow over time like a tree, but it must endure the elements. Anything that grows from the ground, a flower or a tree, will die in isolation. Without water, sunlight, dirt, or other living beings around them like insects, they will not thrive. Yet, if you were under the same conditions as that seed, you may not be so quick to count your blessings. If a seed refused to be placed in the ground for fear of being surrounded by the dirt, nothing would ever grow. It could never reach its full potential and bloom. Here is the key difference. A seed is being planted, not buried. The process looks and feels the same. But if you are being buried, when you are covered in dirt, this is your end, your final resting place. If you are being planted, when you are covered in dirt, this is your beginning, your place to grow. When challenges arise, do you recognize the difference? Understand that many challenges are there to help you grow, just like a seed that needs to be covered in the dirt. The rains will come but rain is not a problem if you know that you are being watered. If you are planting the seeds of your vision, there will come a time when you must rise to the occasion. Approach challenges with the eye of the visionary. Embrace them as an opportunity for you to weather the storm. Even if all you have is a seed, know that there is a tree in the palm of your hand. Grow it so you can rise.

Be Willing to Embrace Your Past

Out of the huts of history's shame, I rise
Up from a past that's rooted in pain, I rise
Bringing the gifts that my ancestors gave,
I am the dream and the hope of the slave.

-Maya Angelou, Still I Rise[xi]

When I was about 12 years old, my parents gave me a book titled *Maya Angelou: Poems* by the great writer. I carried this book around with me for years. Through high school, I learned to recite many of her poems from memory at church and local cultural events. One important lesson I learned from her work was no matter where you are from, what you have been through, or what it took for you to be where you are today, your life matters. Be clear about who you are and rise. Your legacy depends on it. You are standing on the shoulders of giants, picking up where all those who came before you left off. To rise means to acknowledge them and let the marathon continue with you.

Stand up, Be humble. One day, you will reach higher heights. You will do more than your ancestors dreamed. You will be a great and mighty oak tree. But in this season, you are a seedling. A pupil. As a student, you are studying, learning to endure the dirt and weather the storms. But just because you are still developing doesn't mean you don't have anything to contribute. You can still stand up in your situation, knowing that you have plenty more to learn. Be humble enough to ask the questions and receive the wisdom tempered knowledge from mentors. It may seem easier to say, "Well, I will sit down quietly and say nothing until I know more, then I can stand up and lead." But to stand as tall as you can as you learn is a powerful way to show your advisors, mentors, and community members that you are available for on-the-job training. You are ready and willing to contribute what you have right now as the foundation for learning more. You are asking questions and taking notes. You are showing up and showing them that you are a team player, that you are coachable. Don't let not insecurity, fear of failure, or perfectionism convince you not to contribute until you know everything, until it is perfect. Show those who've made an investment in you that you are taking notes and implementing where possible. Lead by example. Be courageous enough to stand up with confidence and humbleness to share what you are learning. Ask questions. Answer questions. Pay attention to what is happening around you. Be willing to demonstrate your growth. You can lead, and you can learn. Let's go!

Reality Check Your Vision: Describe a season in your life that you can compare to a seed growing into a tree? What is the one Rise principle that you need to implement immediately in order to free your real vision?

Chapter 12

VISION TRANSFORMATION: LEAD LIKE A BUTTERFLY

"We delight in the beauty of the butterfly but rarely admit the changes it has gone through to achieve that beauty." – Maya Angelou

Lead With Vision. It's time for you to lead with vision. That means first embrace your role as a leader: a visionary leader. There are some outdated ideas of leadership that hinge on a formal position or a title. The designation of a leader used to be limited to the top: the CEO of a company, the pastor of a church, or an elected official. However, leadership of today is not limited to only those at the top. When leadership is defined by one's character, their ability to collaborate with others, and their demonstration of transformative growth, then leadership becomes more personal than positional. Visionary leaders don't need a specific position; instead, they understand they have been uniquely positioned to lead. Don't wait until you are at the top to think of yourself as a leader. This means you can lead as an administrative assistant and as a mother; as a wife and a womanpreneur. Your life is filled with professional and personal leadership opportunities. Do the internal work, the self-reflection, the personal growth. What did you learn about yourself from that last situation? How have you grown from it? Who are you now and how are you better equipped to thrive in the future? That is what transformation is all about. Nothing demonstrates this process better than a butterfly who has several cycles of change before it receives the colorful wings it is most known for. It is a story of humble beginnings, change, isolation, and resilience. There are aspects of this process that you will relate to more than others. An extrovert might decry the season of isolation while the introvert may completely embrace it but loathe the frequent uncertainty of change. Whichever you are, get what you need. Allow yourself to connect to the aspects of this journey that help you to internally lead your way through seasons of transformation. As a visionary leader, you are a woman with vision and whenever you show up you bring a light and a spark with you everywhere you go.

Be The Butterfly. Back when I was a youth coordinator for an Atlanta non-profit, I visited a garden and nature preserve in rural Georgia, about two hours outside of the city of Atlanta with some middle and high school students. The preserve had a butterfly habitat where hundreds of butterflies in various stages of metamorphosis roamed among the fresh flowers. Watching them in each stage of life was so awe inspiring and strangely beautiful. It was wonderful talking with the students about the different phases, watching them witness transformation right before their eyes. To them, it was like magic or a miracle. That day, learned about the four distinct life cycles of a butterfly: from egg to caterpillar, then chrysalis. And the final stage is the butterfly.

Each season of this process comes with a new look and new skills to navigate the world. It is a constant rebirth and transition from one extreme to the next. It is designed to do this. It is born with just about everything it needs to make the journey from one phase of life to the next, reemerging changed and ready to explore the world. You are like the butterfly, fully equipped to change from one season of life to the next, each time reemerging with new experiences, new gifts, and new skills that make you more beautiful from the inside out. It is incredible how a season of life can take a person like you through a process that changes your very nature by bringing out things you may not have known were there.

It reminds me of a lump of coal that can be transformed into a diamond with the right amount of heat and pressure. When the process is over, that same lump of coal looks completely different and has been changed forever. Yet, the process only revealed what was already there. This was my experience when I decided to go back to college and get an advanced degree, the first in the family to do so. It is how I felt when I fell in love with my husband and when I became a mother. It is how I felt the day I sat down to write this book. In those moments, I was completely transformed. And yet, those experiences only brought out more of me so I could live fully and embrace a real vision of my life.

Now, it's your turn. Embrace your life at every step of the process. Embrace your inner caterpillar with those humble beginnings. Hold your head up high, for those experiences are the preparation for greatness. Embrace your chrysalis and the discomfort, allowing you to dig deeper rather than give up. Embrace the beautiful transformation of the butterfly as just one part of your life's journey.

Honor Your Whole Journey. There's a great deal of attention placed on the beauty of the butterfly. Far less attention is given to the caterpillar and the physical changes it must endure for its incredible journey from egg to chrysalis. If at any point the caterpillar didn't survive, it doesn't become the butterfly. And who pays attention to the chrysalis? Yet, we marvel at the butterfly- the delicate wings, the beautiful colors, and its ability to transform a garden by nurturing flowers. But when you gaze at the caterpillar, do you see all that it has inside? Or do you compare it to a worm? Our society is obsessed with the "before" and "after" picture. Rarely is the "before" picture celebrated. Yet, "after" pictures are worthy of praise and cheers. It ends up being all about the end result. This diminishes the full journey. Many women leaders I have worked with over the years have this same issue, only focusing on the end and short-changing their amazing journey.

No matter where you are or what you have done, there is always a desire to do more. But somehow, doing more quickly translates to feelings of inadequacy as though you haven't done enough. A quick scan of your life can leave you with questions. Ever hear yourself say things like, "I thought I would be further along by now. When are things going to work out for me?" And, "Have I done anything meaningful with my life?" Imagine being a caterpillar on her way to becoming a butterfly. Literally.

Embrace Your Experience. On the journey to becoming a butterfly, there is a point in the process where there is no caterpillar, and there is no butterfly. Isolated from everything familiar, there is only a jellyfish-gooey substance wrapped in a cocoon called a chrysalis. Imagine this. You are locked in darkness, unable to crawl, and cannot fly. You could care less about some wings. All you want to do is to get out; to move freely, to do your own thing. No wings, and no pretty colors. Alone. If I were the caterpillar, here is the part where I would start asking all of the questions while I side-eye all the other caterpillars who told me to just trust the process.

Them: You're going to be a beautiful butterfly someday.

Me: *Listen Linda! Nobody told me in order to get my wings, I would have to look like the blob; shadow of my former self, suspended in mid-air from a tree branch, holding on for dear life. Nothing looks or feels familiar. At this point, forget the wings. They're overrated anyway. I will gladly go back to crawling on the ground as a caterpillar if I can just get out of here. What part of the game is this? I give up!*

When I hear women speak like the caterpillar during workshops, retreats, and coaching sessions, it is so familiar to me. It is a voice, frustrated with change and with self. It is clear to me that this is the same frustrated and disgruntled negative self-talk they speak to themselves in the midst of a challenging situation. But nobody is just waking up one day saying, "How can I talk down to myself today?" From girlhood to grown, women and girls are rewarded for being special in some way. It is validation and confirmation of a job well done. It's equivalent of being ranked "Top 10" in a class, or making the cheerleading squad, or being chosen first when friends are picking teams at recess. No one wants to be chosen last to play, and instead of learning to celebrate the process, the focus is solely on the win. However, just like the caterpillar in the chrysalis, there is more to your journey. The caterpillar had a whole life before it became a butterfly. Honor your whole journey, in its entirety, and embrace all the meaningful experiences that make you exactly who you are.

Affirm Your Journey. Through deeper conversations and assessments, I discover that the women who have talked to me about needing to accomplish more have actually already accomplished amazing things: completed a degree, landed a competitive job, created community projects, been a leader in the church, survived trauma, paid off debt, purchased a home, became a mentor, etc. The list goes on and on. As busy as life can be from one year to the next, it is easy to forget about goals accomplished in what seems like a faraway yester-year. Let me remind you that life is a marathon, not a sprint. Your entire life matters to God; let it matter to you as well. Don't belittle yourself by diminishing all that you've done for yourself and your community. Your leadership has no expiration date, so take the limited timeline and the pressure off. Part of honoring your whole story is remembering what you have already been through. Remember what you have already conquered. Remember who you are. Be empowered by that because it becomes your fuel for creativity and vision as you prepare to endure new stages of your life.

Be Still and Know You Will Be Ok. Difficult circumstances are meaningful, even purposeful, in your life and can help you tremendously. You need to be right here, exactly where you are. What if getting to the other side of this transition and becoming a butterfly is not just something you are going through, but a necessary transformational process that actually helps propel you to the next level? Sometimes, you need to be in a quiet dark place where you will sit still and grow. You need the chrysalis. You are not stuck. You are just not used to sitting still. Try to rest more than you resist. Relax. Relate. Release.

The very thing you are praying for could be found right here, right now in your chrysalis.

Stop Stealing from yourself. President Theodore Roosevelt once said, "Comparison is the thief of joy." So much joy is stolen from life by constantly measuring the quality of your life against someone else's experience you find similar to your own. Comparing is different than learning. Learning asks, "What can I glean and how can I apply it to help me in my own situation?" Comparing asks, "Who is doing better? If I am, then how can I keep doing better than them? If they are, then why are they doing better than me?" But I love how faith and business entrepreneur Lara Casey expands on this in her book:

> "Comparison isn't just the thief of joy, it's the thief of everything. Keep your eyes on your purposeful path. Celebrate others. Celebrate progress, not perfection. Cultivate gratitude over comparison. Gratitude turns what we have into more than enough." -Lara Casey, Cultivate What Matters[xii]

Gratitude for what you have and what you have been through can go a long way in this process. Taking your eyes off others will decrease that jealousy and envy that you secretly experience. Whether you have thought it, said it, or even prayed it, it comes down to this: "Why them and not me?" When you compare your journey to others, you steal from yourself in two ways: magnify and minimize.

#1: **Magnify** – you magnify the success of others into a perfectly edited highlight reel, similar to a famous athlete, full of wins with no fumbles stirring up envy; and you also magnify your challenges turning them into dismal failures.

#2: **Minimize** – you minimize the challenges of others to a seldom anomaly; and you also minimize your own success stories to small happy accidents, diminishing their value and being ungrateful for what you do have.

This process is a disservice to you. It clouds your heart and your vision. It's time to own the lies and be honest with yourself and others. Be honest about what you have really done, not to humble brag or boast, but to paint an honest picture of what God has enabled you to do. It's also time to have a nice reality check about those wonderful superstars you admire so much. I know you know this but, I have to say it anyway. Your favorite has their own baggage they are dealing with and are trying not to compare themselves to someone they admire as well. It's a vicious cycle that throws salt in every wound of unworthiness, every jealous bone, and good ole' fashion envy. This is the opposite of what helps you grow. Don't allow comparison to steal your joy or anything else.

Survive and Thrive. It's time to reframe failure. Celebrate what did not work as information rather than see it as failure. Seize the moment and find the opportunity. After living in New York for a few years, I was ready to move to a city with a slower pace but just as much culture and community. I began applying for positions across the entire country. But my eye was on Atlanta. I had many friends from college there and family nearby in Alabama. When I got the call to do an interview for a college leadership program, I was bursting with excitement. I had the perfect job interview with the perfect company. What had started with 100 applicants was now down to the top five. I just knew the opportunity was mine. So, I moved to Atlanta on a hope and a prayer that it would all work out, as a demonstration to my future employer of how committed I was since they were concerned that I wasn't a local at the time of my first interview. After all, five years prior, when I left Los Angeles for an 8-week internship in Washington, D.C., I took a huge risk leaving a job that was paying my bills, an apartment, and my entire world behind me. *And that worked out great,* I thought. In just two months, I was offered the full-time job and moved to D.C. back then. *This will work out just like before!*

Spoiler alert. It didn't work out just like before. It didn't work out how I envisioned it at all. Suffice it to say, I didn't get the job, and I was devastated. After three interviews and moving across the country to get the job, they decided to promote a current employee instead. To add insult to injury, I later found out the person promoted into that position had actually interviewed me. Talk about a conflict of interest. It felt like a slap in the face. Either way, they had the job, I didn't, and now I needed to move forward. I slept on the couch of some generous friends for a few months until I figured out the next step, which turned out to be a necessary detour on my life path.

When discussing failure, Oprah said, "You either win or you learn." Well, Oprah, that day I learned, and in the long run, it helped me win. It was a surprise to me but not God. Right there, in the midst of my crisis, I started my first business. I started consulting for non-profits and entrepreneurs as a side hustle to supplement my income and pay a few household bills until I found a full-time job. However, I kept the business going even when I got a new job because I felt empowered helping my clients grow their platforms from an idea to implementation. My clients taught me a new definition of success apart from getting a good job.

After years of running my business part-time, I realized that I wanted to be a full-time entrepreneur, running my business and my life on my own schedule, instead of a traditional nine to five career path. With a shift in perspective, what I initially saw as my failure to get a highly competitive job actually turned out to benefit me greatly by setting me on a path to business in ways that I would not have pursued on my own.

Why does failure feel so painful instead of pivotal? As I dig deeper into my own experience, I see that underneath the fear of failure is a word even more cringeworthy: rejection. Instead of taking it in as information, rejection says, "I take this personally." There are times when the job, the relationship, or the friendship just doesn't work out. However, settling on failure and rejection as the end of the epic battle inevitably does not lead to vision, hope, and purpose. It leads to internalized defeat. It can leave you stuck in survival mode as though surviving is all you are here on this earth to do. But sis, you were called to more than that. You are more than your struggles. Therefore, surviving them is a necessary step, but it is not the whole staircase. In order to ascend from surviving to thriving, you will need to reframe the pain, learn whatever lesson you can glean from this, look out for the next right opportunity to move forward, and be determined to do just that.

Reality Check Your Vision: Describe a season in your life that you can compare to the metamorphosis of a butterfly? What is the one Lead principle that you need to implement immediately in order to free your real vision?

Chapter 13

VISION TRANSFORMATION:
SHINE LIKE THE SUN

"If there's one thing I've learned in life, it's the power of using your voice." -Michelle Obama

Shine like the Sun. Did you know that the sun is actually the brightest star? It is powerful. It gives natural light to the world. It provides warmth to the earth. The sun shines bright all year around. Even when it is covered by clouds, you may not be able to see it, the sun still shines. It is consistent, and we depend on the sun more than is acknowledged. Without it, nothing else grows. The sun helps life survive and thrive. There comes a time when you are in a really good place; solid and at peace with God, yourself, and others. This is the warmth. This is the light. This is the sun. It is a season for you to flourish as well as nourish others. It is a season of sharing and serving from a full cup. In fact, your cup runneth over. After you have done the necessary work to rise and lead, it is time to shine. You have been intentional about reflecting, it is your turn to shine and share that joyful warm heart.

Share Your Story. The story you tell yourself about yourself matters. There is a story told all over the world about three men working on a building after a terrible fire. It's based on a real fire in the 17th Century in Europe. The three men were working on the building when the architect walked by and noticed that while the men were doing the same thing, they had different expressions on their faces, and they weren't working at the same pace. Two of them looked like they were ready to quit at any moment. Concerned, the architect asked, "What are you doing?" The first man replied, "I'm a bricklayer so I am building bricks." He asked the second man the same question. "I'm a builder, so I am making a wall for this building." The architect then came around to the third man, the most productive out of the three and said, "What are you doing?" With joy in his voice and a smile, the man replied, "I build cathedrals, and I am here to build a great cathedral to the Almighty God." The architect then made him the head builder to lead the others. What's the story here? All three men were completing the same work, but the difference was the story that they told themselves and others about their purpose. The bigger the why, the greater connection to vision and purpose. Each man had meaning behind their work, but the one with great vision told a vastly different story. Here are two ways for you to lead with your story:

1. **Be Authentic.** Everyone has a story, a pivotal experience, a moment that empowered them to step forward in an intentional way. What is that story for you? It is easier to share a summary featuring details of the experience without sharing the "why." It is just as important to describe what happened as it is to explain why you believe it happened. Personalizing it sets you apart and gives the experience 100% authenticity. It requires you to search your soul a little bit more and make some meaning out of your experience. What did you learn? What surprised you? In what way does this connect to your values? Think about how it is similar or different than other experiences you have had in the past. This also provides the opportunity for people to know you authentically as a person rather than a title or position you occupy. Leading with your story can help you to make meaning out of your life and connect it back to your real vision.

2. **Be Brave:** Your story has power. It is powerful to have a lived experience that you can learn from. It is a powerful choice to share that experience and expertise with someone else, encouraging them to glean from your lessons and apply the wisdom to their own life. This is what it means to lead with your story. It's time to find your voice and the courage to share those humble beginnings, best practices, lessons learned, and even mistakes along the way. Sharing doesn't mean write a "tell-all" book about your life. It is imperative that you establish healthy boundaries and only share when you feel safe to do so. Still,

when you are approached with heartfelt questions, provide a response that is thoughtful, honest, and builds up the relationship of trust. Reaffirm that you are a leader who is comprised of character, values, and powerful experiences that inform a compassionate world view that leads you to serve.

Your Voice Matters. Speaking of saying something powerful, it is important for you to not only share the "what" (the cause) but the "why" as well. Your story of why you are deeply committed to your journey can also motivate and inspire others. By sharing your own story in relationship to an important cause, you can make the real-life connection to elicit empathy and compassion, a prerequisite for others who have a less personal connection to the cause to eventually take some action alongside you. The powerful truth is your age does not matter when your voice matters more. How memorable is Malala Yousafzai, a young leader who survived a violent attack at the age of fifteen and now speaks out against gender-based violence while promoting education for girls? Mari Copeny aka "Little Miss Flint" comes to mind for her work at eight-years-old to increase action and raise awareness about the water crisis in Flint, Michigan. She wrote a letter that led President Barack Obama to come visit her in Flint and meet with local government.

I also love learning about the women of NASA like Katherine Johnson, as told through the film *Hidden Figures,* organized with other women many referred to as "computers" to get higher wages and better working conditions. When the film was first released in theaters, my grandmother Nora went to see it. She asked my sister Lakinda to make plans to see the movie not once, not twice, but at least three times. My sister, the loving caretaker she is, saw the way my grandmother lit up and obliged the request over and over again just to make her grandmother smile. After the third time, I asked my grandmother what made her enjoy the movie so much? She simply said it was a good film with the women working together. Upon the occasion I had to write her obituary, I learned that my grandmother at one time had worked as a "computer" for the IBM Computer corporation in the 1960's. Immediately, it clicked for me why this film was one of such great importance. There was something in that film, something about Ms. Katherine choosing to tell her story, that brought my grandmother, who never told her story, some joy.

Perhaps you are thinking that your story is nothing like that and is less worthy of your voice. Think again. It doesn't have to be a personal story that you connect to a bigger mission. In some cases, it is retelling the stories of others with attention towards centering those most affected that can have just as much power. Think about Alicia Garza, one of the founders of Black Lives Matter from Oakland, California. She heard the story of Trayvon Martin, an unarmed Black teenage boy who was killed in Florida. From one coast to the other, Garza saw her own story intertwined with his and committed to make a difference through policy and protest.

All the activists and trailblazers mentioned have done great work. But this is not limited to them because this is not a story of the meager few. I shine light on their stories to remind all of us that we all have the capability to do the same. There are hundreds of thousands of women who dare to use their voice to influence change in every sphere of society. Creators, entrepreneurs, and faith leaders can raise awareness about issues impacting the community too. Issa Rae used YouTube to tell stories about her experience as a Black woman in the workplace and has now become an advocate for diversity in media. Actress Alyssa Milano joined forces with grassroots organizer, Tarana Burke, to promote the #MeToo movement in an effort to call out sexual violence around the country. I admire folks like Latasha Morrison for creating Be The Bridge, an organization dedicated to addressing diversity and racial reconciliation within Christian churches and communities. You have incredible influence. Use it to say something powerful.

Shine Your Light on a Cause. You can make a difference. As a leader with a vision for yourself and your community, you can make an important contribution to society by adopting a cause. Using your voice for good can help you amplify causes and raise awareness. What is a social cause that is close to your heart? Take a closer look at the issue to see what will help advance the cause locally, nationally, or globally. I guarantee that you will find a number of ways you can contribute to that cause. Whether it is more votes, more volunteers, or more donations, you can make a difference by expanding your platform to include an important cause.

Two causes dear to my heart are increasing access to education for girls and decreasing violence against women. When I moved to Atlanta, I learned about the rise of violence against women and girls in the form of sex trafficking. Georgia, California, New York, and Washington D.C. were all places I'd called home and all places highly ranked in the human and sex trafficking world. My knowledge at the time was more about international problems than anything else based on movies and television. To learn more about the reality of this dire situation, I attended workshops with organizations like YouthSpark in Atlanta dedicated to raising awareness about the sex trafficking of minors in Georgia. It was mind boggling, but it opened my eyes to a thinly veiled world all around me. For a few years, I went on to do advocacy training around this topic with educators, helping them to increase their awareness of the issue and know the warning signs. I also partnered with several organizations to do workshops with middle and high school girls. I had the pleasure of working with several college students who began nonprofit organizations to combat the crisis and rehabilitate girls who had been able to escape that life.

In 2018, when I heard about the complicated and traumatic story of Cyntoia Brown, which made national news, it sounded all too familiar. Cyntoia became the public face for urban sex trafficking of minors with a technique called "boyfriending." At sixteen years old, she was given a life sentence and spent the next sixteen years of her life in prison before the governor of Tennessee commuted her sentence to time served. I took to social media calling for friends, family, and followers to write her letters of encouragement and to help raise funds for her legal fees and re-entry. So many people who didn't know her story said they would write or donate. My heart was so full because it was a powerful reminder that we can be a force for positive change. Upon release, Cyntoia went on to write a memoir. In *Free Cyntoia*, she writes that, in addition to her family, the two things she attributes her ability to survive and thrive in prison under some of the most strenuous circumstances were her access to education, where she received an Associates of Arts degree while in prison, and her faith as she became a Christian while reading her Bible in her cell. In the book, she thanks the many people across the country she never met who prayed for her and encouraged her through this process.

As a collective, we are stronger together. You don't have to have a large following in order to post about a cause on your social media page. Your friends, family, sorority sisters, business club bestie, small group members, and that one friend you haven't seen since high school are a captive audience. Commit to sharing more information on or offline, once a week or once a month. It's really whatever you can commit to actually doing. Ready to take up a cause and be an advocate? Get social! Social media is an effective way to amplify your voice so that your message can shine bright. Get plugged in online through social media regarding social justice and advocacy issues to create a bigger impact. Ready to do more than share information online? Find a local or national organization on the cause and join them! Take a workshop on the topic to find out about best practices on how you can advocate for change.

Celebrate Your Body. Celebrate your journey and your progress in all of its transitions. This body you are in has carried you and that is worthy of celebration. But I didn't always celebrate. As a very tall, curvy, brown skin Black girl, the messages I received about my body from society could be summed up in one phrase: not the one. If you are not the popular one, the one with the name brand clothes, the skinny one, the light skinned one, or the athletic one, I was told by society that "your body doesn't matter." The people with these specific attributes are special. But I was to understand that I was not special, and neither was any BODY else. In high school, I had a dear friend who was partially deaf and wore a hearing aid. I remember a guy we knew explaining to me that she was really pretty, and he wanted to date her, but she was deaf wearing a hearing aid. So, for that reason, he made fun of her instead.

I knew early on that my body was considered a problem. I felt like I was in the way. Growing up, I always sat in the back of the classroom, or in the back of the theatre so I would not "get in anybody's way." I cannot count the number of times I changed my hairstyle, changed my shoes, changed my seat to make others more comfortable because my body was in the way. I used to slump my shoulders so that I would appear shorter and less intrusive. I can still hear my grandmother's voice every Sunday at church. "Shoulders back, chin up, and enunciate your words when you speak." They were the most difficult instructions a girl like me could receive. It took years as an adult to heal, give myself permission to stop hiding, and take up space.

Since elementary school, I have been asked, "How tall are you?" and teased because of it. During the summer between third (3ʳᵈ) and fourth (4ᵗʰ) grade, my mother took me to enroll in an education and arts summer camp. I had attended the previous year, so I was excited to go back. That is until I arrived mid-day during lunch. The entire camp with at least 100 student's 1ˢᵗ-8ᵗʰ grade were seated according to class. My mother walked me over to the counselor as everyone waited to see where the new girl was going. I passed the 8ᵗʰ grade table and the 7ᵗʰ grade table. When I walked past the 5ᵗʰ grade table, I heard the room erupt in gasp and laughter. "Dang, she's a little kid but she's that big?" We continued to walk past the 4ᵗʰ grade table and stopped at the 3ʳᵈ grade kids table. The boisterous laughter got even louder to the point the counselors had to quiet the room. My mother signed the papers with the counselor with plans for me to come back the following day. I never returned. It really hurt my little heart to know that my body was such a joke. We are not conditioned to accept different. I can smile about it now, though. Granted. I did look at least 3 years older than I was, and I was the same height as the camp counselors.

Even as an adult, I am still asked the same question a few times per month followed by a very predictable exchange. It really wouldn't have been overkill for me to walk around with a t-shirt on that said "Taller Than You." Common responses go something like this: "No basketball or modeling? All that height gone to waste." "That's such a waste of talent. If you weren't going to use it, you should have given it to me!"

Surprise, surprise! I started to think of myself as a waste. For years, the frequent comments on my height and body brought out feels of insecurity in many areas of my life. I began to interpret these little conversations, mostly with strangers in line at the grocery store or out on a first date with some random dude, to mean that I was a waste and a bit useless since I clearly did not use my body in the way that everyone saw its intended purpose. I actually had someone tell me that I would be the perfect girlfriend if only I was shorter and thinner. *So, it must be true* I concluded. *I will never fit in.* It was true that I would never fit in. I had to agree that my six-foot-two-inch frame, my dark brown skin, my curly-kinky-nappy hair, my loud voice, and 200+ pound self would never fit in or blend with the crowd. Then I realized that I didn't have to fit in. I was made to stand out. I did not need to shrink down or lose one pound. I didn't need to straighten my hair or wear make-up to lighten my skin. I did not need to step aside and let someone else have all the big dreams and the beautiful life. I decided that with this body, this life was worthy of celebration just as it is. Your body story may be different than mine, but whatever your story, you must reach a place where you do not apologize for your body and you celebrate it instead.

Celebrate EveryBODY. With this new epiphany, more opportunities came for me to talk with other women about their body insecurities. I have grown in the healing of my own body challenges and want to championed other women across the spectrum of age, body type, height, weight, dis/differing ability, and all the many "first" that are still there to conquer. In the eloquent words of actress Lupita N'yango, "No matter where you are from, your dreams are valid." Her words gave me chills as I watched the first-time actress, African immigrant, beautiful dark brown skin, natural hair, Black woman accept her award at the Oscars. But those same words can seem heavy and impossible for a young woman who feels unworthy.

I want to reassure you today that you matter! Your dreams are valid because you matter. Celebrate you. You are worthy right now, no matter what stage you are in. Celebrate you today, not later when you "Get yourself together," or once you get your makeup on. Right now. And then pay it forward. Be the people's champion. You know what you and your body have been through. Use that compassionately to support and encourage others to journey in their bodies as whole people who can always grow, change, and improve. But the changes are not what make them whole or worthy. Celebrate diversity in all its forms. Celebrate those who are different from your walk of life.

Listen & Lead. In Margaret Wheatley's book, *Turning to One Another: Simple Conversations to Restore Hope to the Future*, she says, "We have the opportunity many times a day, every day, to be the one who listens to others, curious rather than certain. But the greatest benefit of all is that listening moves us closer. When we listen with less judgment, we always develop better relationships with each other. It is not our differences that divide us. It's our judgements about each other that do. Curiosity and good listening bring us back together." [xiii]

As simple as it sounds, the inclination of a leader, whether it is a boss, mentor, or parent, is often to speak, direct, and guide. Listening is an act of deep invested interest and curiosity. Being a good listener almost sounds too passive to be described as an action or support. But it's quite the opposite of being passive. Listening can be a very "active" process. Stay engaged, keep listening. Ask the questions that lead to connection of like-minded people and shine a light on others by letting them know their stories matter, too.

Declutter Your Life. Although I like Marie Kondo's book, *The Life-Changing Magic of Tidying Up*, I am not what you might call "tidy." After years of traveling and moving around the country, I learned to live out of a suitcase. After graduating from college in Los Angeles,

California where I was born and raised, I traveled and lived in many places like Washington, DC, New York, Toronto, and Birmingham, Alabama. After a few years, I settled in Atlanta, Georgia. But even though I had been living in Atlanta in the same house for two years, I still pretty much lived out of a suitcase and a duffle bag. You can imagine my shock when I got married and my husband moved in. One of the first things he said to me was, "Wow, you have a lot of stuff." I said, "What? No, I don't! I just have a thing here and a bag there." Turns out, without even noticing, I began a collection of sorts. I even had one room completely dedicated to things that I might use someday. The things I stored included furniture left behind by an old roommate. Why had I kept these things? Why hadn't I pulled them out to the curb on trash day? The truth is that I was afraid. I was afraid that just when I got rid of them, I would need them. I was afraid to let things go for fear that I would be helpless and my needs unmet. Although I had this clear vision of settling down in Atlanta, I was secretly afraid that if I got rid of these things that became symbols of stability –like a kitchen table I never used, an oversized hallway mirror that didn't fit into my hallway, or an unused lamp – it would mean that I was letting go. I equated letting go of these things to letting go of my place in a city that I loved. For me, it felt as if cleaning out my closet was foreshadowing a move to an unknown elsewhere. Besides my hometown, I'd never lived anywhere longer than two years.

When I moved to Atlanta, staying here was not even the goal. My plan was to continue life as a nomad, moving every two to three years to another state or country. Instead, my vision had evolved into one of stability at Station ATL. It became a bit of a home in my heart. As I reflect, I see that I was holding on to the furniture as a way to hold me in place. "See, God, I can't up and move because I have a whole house full of furniture. It's not me and a suitcase anymore." Who was I trying to convince? God already knew the deal. I was still applying for jobs in North Carolina, Louisiana, New York, and DC while I was nesting in my West End apartment. Overtime, though, these things that I was trying to use to hold me into place felt like less of an anchor and more like weights holding me down. I wasn't getting any good use out of them. Instead, they sat in my house taking up space and collecting dust.

Overtime, keeping things I didn't need and didn't want, clouded my vision for a peaceful, artsy home. When I realized this, I made my peace with letting go. I gave away as much as I could to neighbors and people I knew. I sold a few items and donated a great deal to thrift stores in my neighborhood. It changed my life, and I am much more conscious of my attachment to things. I'm no Marie Kondo minimalist, but I do have a few new personal rules. First, I don't accept things that I cannot use immediately. If an item is only useful in the "what if" future, then I can be concerned about getting my needs met once that situation actually happens. Second, I think twice before I buy. Now that I have bought a home with my husband that sits on nearly two acres of land, I must be prudent in my purchases to maintain these healthy habits. If I am not intentional, I could find myself impulse buying things just to fill up the house. That is no longer the goal. Living a life filled with useless stuff does not make me feel secure now. I am no longer using things to anchor me. Instead I am anchored in the intangible. My faith in the Lord and my love for my family anchor me in ways that a kitchen table never could.

Shine Together. There is an African Proverb that says, "If you want to go fast, go alone. If you want to go far, go together." It means that you go further when you are together with those who are traveling along the same path. No more rugged individualism that is so prominent in American culture where you alone pick yourself up by your own bootstraps and climb the ladder of success by sheer will. Alone. I mean, how does one do that anyway? Have you ever tried actually laying on the ground and tugging at your boots to help you stand? For such a popular phrase, it makes zero sense. I need to be able to reach out to another person and get some help getting back up. This might be a scary thought for some. Dozens of women have shared with me that as girls, they were bullied, they didn't fit in, or they just didn't get along with the girls from their school or church. Even as adults, they still have struggles to establish healthy trusting friendships with other women. Too often, women and girls are pitted against each other like we must be in a competition for every man or Marc Jacobs bag out there. We don't have to be. We can value community, even collaboration, over competition. Sis, it's time to get a community of folks who are ready to shine bright with you so you can hype each other up, cheer each other on, hold each other accountable, and share resources for mutual success. When you shine, we all shine!

Use Your S.T.A.G.E. Use your S.T.A.G.E. to cultivate a vision. S.T.A.G.E. stands for skills, talents, abilities, gifts, and energy. You have a stage. Your stage is composed of things that naturally come easy to you and skills you dedicated time and energy to learning along the way. You are already a woman of influence. People are looking up to you, whether you know it or not. Now is the time to shine your light and use all of your amazing attributes for good. Don't let those skills and gifts lay dormant. Your S.T.A.G.E. provides you with a resource to support. Not sure how you can use your gifts for the greater good? Ask yourself "What does my circle or my community keep calling me for?" Show up and shine! Assist where you can, and I promise you will learn something meaningful about how you can use your S.T.A.G.E. in service to your vision. You have them for a purpose. Use them purposefully.

Reality Check Your Vision: Describe a season in your life that you can compare to the clouds parting as the sun shines bright? What is the one Shine principle that you need to implement immediately in order to free your real vision? What cause do you care deeply about?

Chapter 14

NOT YOUR AVERAGE VISION BOARD

You are not your vision board. You were made to do more than manifest a carbon copy of artificial images. Value your journey of a lifetime. It is a rich tapestry of your history, your joys, your sorrows. Your journey. It has to be yours in order for it to be real. #FreeYourRealVision

-Alexandria @YesSheLeads

The average vision board is a projection of what people may dream of without any real connection to what they work towards daily. Some vision boards are just pretty pictures that solely focus on the material rewards society tells you to want. But it doesn't work to buy someone else's vision of you and stick it on a board with glue. The glue is you. You do that by customizing your board and including things beyond material goals. Designing a real vision board with the most significance and authenticity means you will include things that excite your senses and imagination. Focus on things that make you feel hopeful about life; things that make you feel joyful; things that energize you; things that remind you to pursue faith, hope, and love; and things you actually enjoy. This instruction may sound a little "Captain Obvious" to you, but it's not. Be sure that every image you select has a personal message just for you. If there is an image of a happy couple posted on a regular vision board, it can have various meanings. On a real vision board, the only meaning that matters is what it means to you. Which statement best reflects your vision?

#1 I am ready for a relationship

#2 I want to be happier in my existing relationship

#3 I desire marriage

#4 I want to enjoy dating again

A real vision board is personalized. Your vision is *not* a grand illusion of what someone else expects your life to be. It has to be yours in order for it to be real.

Benefits of a Real Vision Board. Why create a vision board? While it's not a magic remedy, it does have many benefits. A vision board is often the first time that many women have sat down to articulate what they want their life to look like. Creating a vision board can be a clarifying process. Continuing your journey of self-awareness and discovery with weekly activities throughout the year can help you to sustain that clarity.

Real vision boards provide you with a daily visual reminder of your dreams and goals. As you take actions to support your dream and turn it into reality, you begin preparing to receive that life. It can help you create short-term goals needed to ascend to long term goals. It involves doing the work to elevate your expectations, change your mindset, and transform your life. It invites others to sow into your vision as you courageously share it with your trusted circle of support who will cheer you on in love and excitement as you transform.

Vision boards make you think about what it is you *REALLY* want. They serve as a regular reminder to imagine and reimagine your giant life. Vision boards are also a creative way to let you express your vision. So often, our desires have been crushed or squelched by life, the pervasive noise of the news and media, and our own experiences, that it is hard to express what we want. Vision helps you learn to express yourself. Vision is about the seen and the unseen, working together to create reality.

Real Vision Board Pre-Work: The following activities are designed for you to complete before you start a new vision board. These activities teach you how to start an authentic and powerful vision board by beginning the process before you focus on the images.

Vision & Values. Vision and values work together. Your values inform your choices and affirm your vision. If your values are strong, and you use them to guide your decisions, then your vision remains rooted to your reality every day. It will never be far.

Step 1- Read over the list of core values below. Underline all the words that are most important to you, words that are essential to your being. You may feel as though you value every attribute on this list; however, you are in search of your core values- the guiding principles that are at the center of your decision-making, your character, and the way you design your life.

Tip: if you must think about it for longer than 3 seconds, then move on; your core values often have a strong immediate impact when you see them or say them. If there is a word that you would like to add, fill it in the blank at the bottom of the list.

Accountability	Curiosity	Home	Openness	Service
Achievement	Dignity	Honesty	Optimism	Simplicity
Adaptability	Diversity	Hope	Order	Spirituality
Adventure	Environment	Humility	Parenting	Sportsmanship
Altruism	Efficiency	Humor	Patience	Stewardship
Ambition	Equality	Inclusion	Patriotism	Success
Authenticity	Ethics	Independence	Peace	Teamwork
Balance	Excellence	Initiative	Perseverance	Thrift
Beauty	Fairness	Integrity	Personal-	Time
Being the best	Faith	Intuition	fulfillment	Tradition
Belonging	Family	Job security	Power	Travel
Career	Financial-	Joy	Pride	Trust
Caring	stability	Justice	Recognition	Truth
Collaboration	Forgiveness	Kindness	Reliability	Understanding
Commitment	Freedom	Knowledge	Resourcefulness	Uniqueness
Community	Friendship Fun	Leadership	Respect	Usefulness
Compassion	Future-	Learning	Responsibility	Vision
Competence	generations	Legacy	Risk taking	Vulnerability
Confidence	Generosity	Leisure	Safety	Wealth
Contentment	Giving back	Love	Security	Well-being
Contribution	Grace	Loyalty	Self-discipline	Wholeheartedness
Cooperation	Gratitude	Making a-	Self-expression	Wisdom
Courage	Growth	difference	Self-respect	**Write your own:**
Creativity	Harmony	Nature	Serenity	_____
	Health			_____

Step 2-Now that you have selected all the words that resonate with you, narrow them down. Give yourself a little bit more time to do this step. Select just five with the most significance that define your character. Do your best to be authentic and actual rather than aspirational. Remember, the values that you select are to be how you engage with the world and what is of the utmost importance in your life.

Tip: Need help narrowing the field? You may have selected words that share similar meanings. Choose what best describes the word in relation to your vision. For example, generosity and giving back are values that are closely related. However, generosity is more along the lines of lavish, unrestricted giving; whereas giving back is focused on replenishing a resource or helping others because of the support that you have already received. Notice how the subtle difference can add meaning and context to your vision. During this exercise, take the time to look up the meaning of your word choices as you narrow them down.

Step 3-Complete the following statements by adding your 5 core values below:

1) I am a woman who_____

2) I am a woman who_____

3) I am a woman who_____

4) I am a woman who_____

5) I am a woman who_____

Create Your Real Vision Manifesto

Step 1: Read and complete each sentence-stem to create the foundation for your Real Vision Manifesto. A manifesto is similar to a declaration or announcement.

I have always had a heart for_____

I believe that_____

My faith empowers me to _____

I really care about _____

I am deeply committed to _____

The values most important to me are _____

I want to see more _____
and I pledge to the students, parents, and teachers in my educational environment that I will do everything I can stay engaged in this effort.

I show up and shine most when I am talking
about _____

What's most important to me is _____

I am dedicated to _____

I will become more _____
so that I can serve my community better.

_____ means so much to me
and I know how important it is for everyone.

I value _____

God has directed me to _____

I see the injustice in _____

Step 2: Now, it's time to make your Real Vision Statement. Make it your own by personalizing it in the following ways:

➢ Decide which sentences represent you best. You can use one or all of the statements in the above activity.

➢ Rearrange the order of the sentences until they flow like you most prefer

➢ Include at least one "I am a woman who…" sentences from the Vision & Values section

➢ Use affirmative present tense statements like "I will…" and avoid conditional word qualifiers such as "I hope to in the future…" or "If things work out, I'll try…."

➢ Add any additional sentences of your own to ensure everything that is important to you is included

➢ Optional: Include a favorite guiding scripture, quote, or affirmation at the end of your statement

Write Your Real Vision Statement Below

What Kind of Vision Board Can I Create?

Personal. Create a lifestyle vision board for yourself. Your vision board can include familiar topics like career, travel, wardrobe, health, romance, and finance. To personalize it even more, consider answering a few additional questions:

"What do I want to learn?"

"What is the message I want to share with others?"

"Who is the community that I want to serve?" "How can I strengthen my faith and grow spiritually?"

"What inspires me to create?"

Add all the other areas of your life that are most important to you if not previously mentioned.

Business. Create a vision board for your business. Whether you desire to be a six-figure solo entrepreneur, or you want to be a CEO on a company managing a staff, you can create a vision board focused on building out a vision for your life in that role. Include the long-term career milestones you want to hit. Don't forget to add your "why" for this goal, such as the lifestyle changes you desire (i.e. more money to travel, more time with family, more flexibility to work from home, more impact in the community).

Couples. Create a vision board for couples. Want to add more romance or celebrate with relaxing vacations and more downtime? This exercise is a clever way to express what you really want out of the relationship. This is also the fun way to do it. It's not just the pictures but the conversations that you can have with it. Imagine the intimacy of sharing the meaning behind your vision, desires, and dreams with each other. You can do a board together that reflects your mutual values, desires, and interests. What's working well? Praise those areas of your love and show gratitude for their continued success. What is missing? This is a key opportunity to call into this void and fill it with an optimistic open heart. Every year since we got married, my husband Jay and I do a vision board. It started with my sharing a favorite hobby with him; but now it is a tradition we both are excited to share.

Family. Create a family vision board with your household. Include the kids and have them create ideas for your lives together as a family. For this, I would suggest a large and thick poster board like a tri-fold presentation poster board. Give your children room to be creative. Help them cut out images that they want to represent themselves or the family with child safe scissors. They can add hobbies they enjoy, places they want to visit, and their favorite foods.

Community Organization. Create a vision board for your church, membership, or community organization. This is a great opportunity to bring people together who are dedicated to a similar cause and provide a space for collaboration. It is an opportunity for many voices to be heard in an inclusive manner. This activity worked well with the Women's Committee of a multigenerational church I worked with in Atlanta who had some generational divides. After diving into the mission and vision statements of the church, each woman selected a word, phrase, image, or scripture that was of utmost significance to her as a woman of faith. Each woman was also able to share why it was important which provided a wonderful bonding experience. Together, they created a beautiful vision board that represented their values and their goals as a community of women.

10 Steps To Making a Real Vision Board. This process is meant to show you how to make an intentional and purposeful vision board that is tailored to you and honors your real vision.

1) Set the tone for this experience. Give yourself ample time to really dive in deep. Set aside two to four hours to complete. Light some nice scented candles. Grab your favorite mug for some coffee, tea, or your favorite beverage. Make a playlist of upbeat and uplifting music you enjoy. Satisfy your sense of sound and have some fun with this.

2) Solo or Group Goals. Decide if you need to work individually or if this is more of a group activity. This can be a solo journey if you need solitude and focus. Want some company? Gather your good-good girl friends who are on a similar journey. Invite them over or host a virtual meet up to share your boards with each other.

3) Choose Your Board. Choosing a board is a really important step. Over the years, I have used various types of vision boards from traditional posters, to a notebook cover, to a photo album. In the age of the internet, some people prefer a virtual board housed on an app or website. What works best for you?

4) Visual Design. – How do you want to add visuals? A free-flowing board like a collage will have pictures that overlap and are situated in no particular order. Whereas, a segmented vision board will have designated sections divided by lines for each area of focus. Example: upper left-hand corner is for health and wellness; lower right-hand corner is for career, etc.

5) Choose your board. Decide on a permanent or progressive board. A permanent board is one that will be complete by the end of your vision board session. The images won't change until you decide to sit down and do another vision board. That can be one year later, or it can be five years later if you feel the content of the board still applies to your vision. A progressive board, on the other hand, is one that you will revisit as often as necessary to add an image or remove one. For a progressive style, an office-size cork board or magnetic board, or a virtual app will be easiest for this versatile style.

6) Get supplies for your vision board – You will need scissors to cut out images and words. I recommend glue sticks versus glue from a bottle to keep the images smooth and reduce lumps. It

is beneficial to have at least one magazine from four different genres to give you access to a variety of images and topics.

7) Get your images. Casually flip through the pages of the magazines and tear out any pages that have a word or image that speak to you immediately. If you have to second guess if you really like a certain image, leave it there and move right along. Don't waste any energy on picture FOMO (fear of missing out). There is plenty for you to choose from. The reality is there are usually an abundance of things that you connect with, not a lack of them. I suggest you turn the page and keep an eye out for images that immediately resonate with you. Just in case you want to come back to it, fold down the edge of the page so you can find it easily again if it is still on your mind.

8) Review Your Collection. Once you have searched through four to five magazines, stop, and review the images that you have. Decide if you have a solid collection that is representative of your vision. After you have pulled all your images and you review them, if you are still thinking of a specific image, then return to it, cut it out, and add it to your existing images. Sort images into common sub-topics. Look at each group of images and select the one that stands out to you the most in that grouping to be the foundational images that start your board. You will design the rest of your board around them by adding more images and words from this starting point. From there, continue adding images until you feel the board is a reflection of your vision, values, and desires.

9) Don't overcrowd your board. There is no pressure to fill up the entire space you have. In fact, you do not need to use every image that you have selected. I have seen beautiful vision boards with five images on them. I have also seen vision boards

with thousands of images. The boards with thousands of images can be difficult to personalize with the techniques described in this real vision board process.

10) Include meaningful words on your vision board. It is important to include words to summarize or offer meaning to your images. You can cut out words that resonate with you from the magazine or write them on your board with color markers. If you are using a poster board, you can have your collage be the focal point at the center and leave room to write a personal message to yourself on the edges.

Post Your Vision Board. After you have created your vision board, select a place to put your board. I like to put it someplace visible and accessible so that I can see it frequently for inspiration and review it as needed. Schedule a time weekly to review your vision statements that you wrote for each image and look at your vision board as a touch point to reflect on your vision in progress. Want to post your board virtually? Share your vision board on social media and use the hashtag #FreeYourRealVision

Reality Check Your Vision: Post Real Vision statement in a visible place where you can see it daily. Read your Real Vision statement out loud to yourself in the mirror. What emotions come up for you? How does this exercise make you feel?

Chapter 15

VISION IN PROGRESS

"Excellence is not a singular act; it's a habit. You are what you repeatedly do." -Aristotle

A vision is different from a goal or a task. However, there is a relationship between the three. Once you get clear on your vision, you can set your goals, and then identify your task. Having a real vision for your life can impact your long-term and short-term goals. I want to encourage you to think big about the vision for your life- the long panoramic view. Goals and vision complement one another when created intentionally. Tasks and habits are useful in a world obsessed with being busy. Being busy does not always equal being productive. Productivity only matters when it is meaningful and purposeful. Increased pressure at work lead many to skip a legally allotted lunch break, sick leave, or vacation time for fear they will look less dedicated to the job. It's no surprise that getting goals accomplished is a top priority. Time management and project management are highly requested professional development trainings for many employers, even though there are literally hundreds of tools out there online. The following tools listed in this chapter are meant to show you what has worked for me, but this is not an exhaustive list. And it is important that you don't try to implement all of these at once. In fact, as you read through each one, underline only two tools you want to focus on trying out. The key is finding what works for you. There is no "one size fits all." Commit to trying two and see if they work for you. Check in on your progress regularly, so you can make the necessary adjustments along the way until you find the tools that work best.

The Purpose of Planning to "Goal" Get It. Planning is an imperfect process that gets better with progress. In the past, struggles with perfectionism fueled my disappointment with planning and goal setting. *Why bother with planning if it's not going to work out the way I planned it?* If you are having a similar thought, I suggest you try driving a car with no mirrors. Do you ever check your side and review mirrors when you drive? Only every single time you drive, right? Of course, you do! But even with mirrors there are still places that you cannot see known as blind spots. Mirrors are a pretty important tool for successful driving. They may not be a perfect solution, but they are proven to help you safely navigate your journey. They help you determine when it is safe to get over when you change lanes, when you need to speed up, or how quickly you need to slow down. Even with the blind spots, it is better to have them in place and use them as needed than to ride along the roads without them. Plans are like having the mirrors in your car. You can work without them, but you can navigate so much better with them in place. There are surprises in life that seem to appear out of nowhere because they have been sitting in a blind spot that you cannot see, and therefore, cannot be planned. At times, this will cause you to adjust your plans. At least you are not starting from scratch. Be flexible. Adapt. Grow.

Goal setting and planning are great tools that can help you incrementally develop your life to match your vision. You can plan for the day, the week, the month, the quarter (every 3 months), and the year. Those who love project management advise making plans using all of the above to create a life sequence where annual planning inform the weekly goals. I must admit, the way my life is set up as a mom and wife with a family business, clients, as well as my work with college students, it can be tough to anticipate plans more than a few months away. However, I am here to tell you that the years I have been able to plan ahead have yielded more success versus the years that I did not. The key is to be flexible and find a style of planning that works for you and your busy lifestyle. In this chapter, I will share some tools that have worked well for me over the years; they help me to see the connection between daily tasks and my future vision. You may find that other tools work better for you, and that is absolutely wonderful. Using the hashtag #FreeYourRealVision share with other visionaries the tools that work for you.

How to be a Goal-Getter. Are you ready to goal-get-it? Did you know you can have a goal for every part of your life? There are two types of goals you need to consider if you are going to be a goal-getter:

Habit Goals

Habit goals are things you want to incorporate into your regularly scheduled life. They have a start date but don't necessarily have an end date, because they are typically on-going. An example is, "I want to drink more water every day." "I want to increase the amount of fruits and veggies I eat daily." "I want to give up smoking." Goals like these are designed to form new habits around your everyday living and can be incorporated into your daily habits. What is one habit-based goal that you would like to incorporate?

Task Goals

Task goals are things that you want to accomplish, which require a list of action steps or tasks, in order to complete. An example is you saying, "I want to get my affairs in order." To accomplish this goal, your tasks might be three-fold:

1. "I want to get a will or living trust."
2. "I want to buy life insurance for my family." '
3. "I want to organize all the important medical documents and put them in one digital file."

Then, once you have completed all the task on your list, that is when you know you have achieved the goal. What is one task-based goal that you would like to accomplish?

How to use SMART Goals.

The best goals are made when you combine the habits you want to create and the tasks you want to accomplish; then together, they can be turned into a S.M.A.R.T. goal. This tool helps you to make goals specific, measurable, achievable, realistic, and time bound. This concept was introduced in the 1950's by Peter Drucker and popularized in the 1990's by George T. Doran, both of which were management and business consultants.

Turning a Habit into a Smart Goal.

Habit: Drink more water.

Goal: "I will drink one gallon of water every day before I go to bed for the next 90 days."

Even though it's a habit, placing a timeline on it makes you able to measure your progress, see if you are being effective, or determine if you need to make changes. It also gives you an off ramp to make a new choice. So, in 90 days, you can evaluate your progress and either set a new short-term goal by adding 90 more days or say, *Hey, I have successfully incorporated this habit into my life. I can move forward trusting myself to just do it from now on.*

Turning a Task into a Smart Goal.

Task: Buy a new professional wardrobe.

Goal: "I will take 25% of my tax refund within thirty days of receiving it and purchase one custom tailored suit and four new professional outfits for work to refresh my wardrobe."

If a lump sum does not work for you, then modify and make it "achievable" for you. Make it smart, but also make it your own. You want this to work. The best part about a S.M.A.R.T. goal is that it is designed for success. Sure, get out of your comfort zone. But this is not supposed to be so much of a stretch that it doesn't get accomplished. It can be incremental or all at once. How about this new adjusted goal?

New Goal: "For the next three months, every pay period, I will purchase one professional outfit to refresh my wardrobe."

The best tasks-oriented goals contain several related tasks that contribute to a broader goal. It implies a lifestyle change and includes many areas that will fall under submission to one goal. Let's take the last example of the wardrobe. What if in addition to an updated wardrobe, there was a goal to get a promotion or a new job? Then it would make sense to have a list of other tasks that can position you for success. Other tasks that could be added into this goal could be to revamp your resume, take an online certification class in your field, attend an industry conference, or update your LinkedIn profile with all of that relevant experience. Each task needs to have a timeline or other measurements of guided implementation. But they can all be interconnected and feed into your goal. That goal can lead to fulfillment of your real vision. Let's connect the dots.

Habits – daily search for jobs, update Linked In, attend professional networking events

Task- update resume and send out 10 per week with cover letters, send out email to my professional circle informing them of the job search, attend mock interview practice, be on time and dress for success at all interviews, notify references

Short Term Goal – get five job interviews for ideal positions and land a job offer in forty-five days with a 20% pay increase; get a promotion within one year and train two junior staff; volunteer one day per month

Long Term Goal – become VP of my division in five years; get six to eight years of experience before launching my own firm and dominating in a competitive industry.

Now, let's connect this all back to vision:

Real Vision Statement- to be successful in all I do; to have a continuously advancing career where I work from the bottom up to make an impact and influence the direction of the industry I am in; to have financial security set as a foundation and take calculated financial risk; to build meaningful relationships with colleagues and mentor the next generation of young leaders in my field; to use my skills, talents, gifts, and abilities to be recognized as a powerful contributor in the field by peers and competitors, to humbly learn from other leaders and reinvest that knowledge into my own family legacy.

Goal-Getter Tools You Can Use

12 Week Year System. After some trial and error, blending planning tools on my own, I found out about the 12-week year planning method spelled out in the book, *The 12-week Year* by Brian Moran. Instead of annual planning, Moran encourages you to do four 12-week deep dive planning sessions per year to stay on track. Then you use goal setting to determine the weekly planning of tasks you need to accomplish each week in order to meet the goal in three months. This method works well for me because it narrows the scope of time that I am focusing on a particular goal to just 12 weeks verses traditional annual planning which is 52 weeks. From there, I take those goals and divide them into weekly and monthly plans. The weekly list gives me a list of tasks to draw from to determine my daily activities which help me stay on task and reach the goals.

In addition to teaching the planning method, Moran introduced me to the idea of holding myself capable rather than accountable. It's less about asking "What *should* I do?" and more about asking "what *capacity do I have to take action today?*" Only you determine what you are capable of doing, so once you determine that, it is exactly what you are responsible for doing. This system encourages you to measure your actions versus measuring the outcomes. I find this to be a much more compassionate approach to success and goal setting. You are capable.

Progressive Planning. Another tool I found helpful in cultivating an action plan around your long-term vision is progressive planning. This is where you write the vision you have in each area of your life, document where you are right now in said area, and forecast where you want to be in the years to come: 1-3 years, 3-5 years, and 5-10 years. Then use those milestones to plan and identify what is needed to get from point A to point B and bridge the gap. Here is an abbreviated worksheet from my vision board workshop that focuses on a 1-5-year plan.

Progressive Planning & Goal Setting

Aspect of Life Assessment	Where I am right Now	Where I *will* be in 1-3 Year	Where I *will* be in 3-5 Years
My Daily Life: city location, free time, hobbies, home/apartment			
My Career: paid work, outlet for professional passions			
My Health: Overall wellness, food & diet, exercise, doctor apt			
My Money: financial planning, budget, debt, credit, savings, investments			
My Faith/Personal Reflection: religious or spiritual practice, personal growth, meditation			
My Relationships: family, friendships, partners, social life			

Time and Productivity Hacks: Use these tools to help you keep track of your time and increase productivity so you can stay focused and achieve your goals.

Use Your Tech to Stay on Track. I am a low-to-no tech kind of girl. So, when discussing planning for me, it needs to be simple to do and easy to remember. There are three (3) easy ways you can use your phone and other accessible technology to help you accomplish your goals.

Use an App. Apps are a billion-dollar business and the good people of Asana, Trello, Slack, and Basecamp get their fair share. There is no perfect app. Everything works as long as you do the work. The key differences are in what you specifically need to maintain clarity and flow:

- capturing notes vs assigning tasks
- working solo or with a team
- app integration into other tools
- using mostly for personal life, work, or business

The bottom line comes down to the amount of details that are needed in this area of your life. If you are a micro-thinker and believe lots of details bring clarity while working with a team, you will want to stay closer to the more comprehensive apps that include workflows, deadlines, prioritizations, and assignments. Apps like Asana or Teams might work for you. If you are a macro-thinker and want to document the general idea you want to share or want to refer back to at a later date, then Slack, Trello, or Google Keep will work great for you.

Be In Sync. Sync your email calendar to your phone calendar with at least three alarms that ring prior to the deadline. It is the worst feeling when I have something important saved in my phone and the alarm goes off ten minutes before I need to be there. Here is what has helped me. I like to use the 1-1-1 rule. At the moment I schedule an appointment, I set it in my calendar IMMEDIATELY and add a reminder for 1 week before, 1 day before, and 1 hour before the appointment. My phone automatically adds the 10 minute before feature. This works well especially with planning ahead. With each reminder, I can complete tasks related to final preparation. If a schedule conflict comes up by the 1 week reminder, I can take that opportunity to reschedule with plenty of advance notice rather than scrambling to figure out how to force it all to work, just to end up cancelling the day before anyway. This could also be a great time to send out an inquiry with a personal appointment for brunch with a friend to see if you two are still confirmed for the time, date, and place that has been set. There is nothing like getting dressed, in the car, leaving the house when you text "On my way to meet you. Be there in 20 minutes" and get "OMG I forgot" reply back. Avoid this entire mood.

Tick, Tick, Tick...TIME! You have a timer. Use it! You can use your timer to help keep you on task. You can use the one on your cell phone or keep a timer device at your desk. Have you ever stopped working "for a minute to take a break?" Then, you look up and an hour has gone by? Where did the time go? You can use your timer to give yourself the social media break you want without getting stuck in the rabbit hole of scrolling for one hour, thinking it was only twenty minutes. Is this just me or nah? The same goes for binge watching a show when you said you were going to give yourself two episodes, then three hours later, half the day is gone. The alarm from the timer can be a good reality check. You can also use your timer for timed task assessments to see where you need to make adjustments. This can tell you how long a task really takes versus how long you planned for help you avoid constantly rushing to get things done. Once, I did a timed task assessment that and realized I was allotting myself one hour to complete a three-hour task. It was a game changer. From then on when I had to complete similar tasks, I gave myself the appropriate amount of time to finish rather than rushing and expecting it to all be done. Your timer is here for you!

Pomodoro Technique[xiv]. I was introduced to the Pomodoro timer in graduate school. It is a more elevated version of the timer method because it comes with a book and productivity instructions. The timer looks like a tomato, reminiscent of an old school oven timer in an episode of *The Brady Bunch*. When you are trying to level up, make sure you have friends that will help you in the process and introduce new tools to get the job done. My friend Fayola got the timer to help me while I struggled to finish my graduate thesis. If you have never heard of the pomodoro tomato, then let me explain. The Pomodoro Technique is a time management technique that uses a timer to break down work into intervals, traditionally twenty-five minutes in length, separated by short breaks. Each twenty-five-minute interval Francesco Cirillo called a pomodoro, the Italian word for tomato. Ironically, a tomato kitchen timer is exactly what you get in the mail if you were to order this system. However, you can simply set your cell phone timer for twenty-five minutes instead, which is just as effective but maybe not as cute. At the end of each interval, you have a five (5) minute break to stretch, return text messages, or get a snack. This is a great time management tool to help you stay focused and on track. With the timer, the idea is to stay completely focused on one thing, no distractions for the entire twenty-five minutes. Unless it is an emergency, don't take a phone call. Don't even get up to use the bathroom. With built in breaks, you can better manage distractions and minor interruptions. It can put the mind to ease and help you focus knowing that in less than a half hour, you will return that text message and scroll social media again to discover that the world is still there where you left it since you last checked your Facebook and Instagram stories.

Reality Check Your Vision: Complete the Progressive Planning and Goal Setting Chart. As you review it, write down what stands out or surprises you most from this exercise. What two (2) Time & Productivity Hacks did you underline to help increase your focus?

Chapter 16

RELEASE YOUR REAL VISION

You are on time for your life! Take the vision that you have right now, however big or small you think it might be, and nurture that. Water that. Let that seed grow into a forest of dreams that turns into reality.

#FreeYourRealVision

-Alexandria @YesSheLeads

Congratulations! You are a ready to release with vision. During this journey together, you learned what it means to have a real vision, not just a vision beholden to the vision board, or a vision bound to societies standards of you. You have broken free from those unrealistic expectations of vision and see clearly where you have access. No more over the top expectations that make vision seem like something only attainable by a special few. As a result, you are ready now more than ever to release your fears, let go of insecurity, challenge those limiting beliefs, and accomplish your goals in order to transform your life. I hope you return to your favorite chapters again and again to reminder yourself to embrace that giant life of yours. Refer back to your highlights and the notes in the margins. Read over your Reality Check Your Vision journal responses. There is so much here and my dear, it is all for you! Ready for next steps? Here are a few things you can do to continue building on your progress!

Schedule Your Personal VIP Meeting: Get ready for your Vision In Progress (VIP) meeting where you take time on a regular schedule to check in on your vision and goals, chart your progress, and update any new developments along the way. Choose how often you will have this VIP meeting with yourself based on your schedule. It can be as frequently as once a month. I do not suggest it exceeds once every 6 months. During your VIP meeting, it is important to pray about your vision. Pray for clarity, direction, and courage to carry on. Then, take some time to write down what you have accomplished in service to your vision in progress since the last meeting. Keep a record of this from one meeting to the next in a journal or notebook so that you can see the ways you are building momentum. I recommend getting a vision book, a journal dedicated to you and your vision. In this book, for every image on your vision board, write down what it means to you and why you selected it. As I mentioned before, two people can have added the same photo to their vision board for completely different reasons. It also creates a deeper sense of clarity as you place goals and actions around your vision. Now, it's time to plan your next set of short-term goals based on your long-term goals you identified in the Progressive Planning and Goal-Setting Worksheet. Last, but not least, share it with a capability partner. A capability partner is someone who can help you hold yourself accountable to accomplishing your goals because they want to see you win and be successful. If this person is on a similar journey, then be sure to hold them capable as well.

Get Your Free Guide. Go to www.yessheleads.com/free-yourrealvision to get your free guide with bonus content and work-sheets that accompany this book!

Host a Real Vision Circle. You can host a Real Vision Circle which is an intimate gathering of friends (2-20 people) where you all can get together, discuss your favorite chapters of this book, and create your Real Vision Boards using the instructions in Chapter 14. During this time together, you can create the space for you and your community to take vision to the next level in your lives with critical support from other women on a similar journey.

Join the Yes She Leads Community. This is a virtual community for you to connect with women dedicated to leading a life that they love with vision. This Facebook group is a community of women who encourage each other, hold each other capable, and speak from a spiritual, healthy, and empowered place. Go to www.yessheleads/fbgroup

REFERENCES

[1] Andersen, Hans Christian. "The Butterfly Sommerflugen" from The Hans Christian Andersen Centre andersen.sdu.dk/vaerk/hersholt/TheButterfly_e.html April 15, 2020

[1] Lexicon by Oxford Dictionary. Vision. https://www.lexico.com/definition/vision May 13, 2020

[1] Rees, Dee. "Pariah." 2011

[1] Hawkins, Tramaine. "The Potter's House," *All My Best to You.* 1991

[1] Hanson, Erin. Untitled. www.instagram.com/thepoeticunderground/

[1] Gilbert, Elizabeth. Big Magic: Creative Living Beyond Fear, Riverhead Books, 2015

[1] Bone, Peter J. Achieve The Impossible: Be Inspired, Challenged, and Equipped to Achieve Your Impossible Dreams. Achieve the Impossible, Pty Ltd, 2019

[1] Maroutian, Emily. www.maroutian.com

[1] **Song, Kelyn. "She started acting at 88. Four years later, she's recognized everywhere for 'Black Panther.'" Washington Post, March 23, 2018**

[1] Moran, Brian and Michael Lennington. The 12 Week Year. John Wiley & Sons, Inc. 2013

[1] Angelou, Maya. "Still I Rise," The Complete Poetry. Random House, 2015

[1] Casey, Lara. Cultivate What Matters: A Grace-Filled Guide to Growing An Intentional Life. Thomas Nelson, 2017

[1] Wheatley, Margaret. Turning To One Another: Simple Conversations to Restore Hope to the Future. Berrette-Koehler Publishers, 2009

[1] Cirillo, Franceso. The Pomodoro Technique. Random House, 2006

ABOUT THE AUTHOR

Alexandria is an author and subject matter expert on leadership, education, personal, and professional development. Through her women's organization Yes! She Leads, Alexandria teaches women how to lead a life they actually love through vision, faith, engagement, and empowerment. As a leadership consultant, Alexandria's portfolio includes keynotes and workshops where she has trained thousands of leaders from nonprofit, small business, collegiate, faith-based, and women's organizations. A ray of sunshine originally from Los Angeles, CA, Alexandria lives in Atlanta raising a little Georgia peach of a daughter Imani with her husband Gerald and her sister Diamond.

Follow & Connect Alexandria on the following pages:

Website: www.yessheleads.com

LinkedIn www.linkedin.com/in/alexandrialeads

Instagram @YesSheLeads

Twitter @YesSheLeads

Facebook @ www.yessheleads.com/fbgroup to join the #SheLeader Community

Made in the USA
Columbia, SC
13 July 2020

13825151R10085